Bosnia and Herzegovina
From Recovery to Sustainable Growth

D1452283

The World Bank
Washington, D.C.

World Bank Country Studies are among the many reports originally prepared for internal use as part of the continuing analysis by the Bank of the economic and related conditions of its developing member countries and of its dialogues with the governments. Some of the reports are published in this series with the least possible delay for the use of governments and the academic, business and financial, and development communities. The typescript of this paper therefore has not been prepared in accordance with the procedures appropriate to formal printed texts, and the World Bank accepts no responsibility for errors. Some sources cited in this paper may be informal documents that are not readily available.

The World Bank does not guarantee the accuracy of the data included in this publication and accepts no responsibility whatsoever for any consequence of their use. The boundaries, colors, denominations, and other information shown on any map in this volume do not imply on the part of the World Bank Group any judgment on the legal status of any territory or the endorsement or acceptance of such boundaries.

The material in this publication is copyrighted. Requests for permission to reproduce portions of it should be sent to the Office of the Publisher at the address shown in the copyright notice above. The World Bank encourages dissemination of its work and will normally give permission promptly and, when the reproduction is for noncommercial purposes, without asking a fee. Permission to copy portions for classroom use is granted through the Copyright Clearance Center, Inc., Suite 910, 222 Rosewood Drive, Danvers, Massachusetts 01923, U.S.A.

Cover photographs by SFOR photographer in Bosnia and Herzegovina.

ISSN: 0253-2123

Library of Congress Cataloging-in-Publication Data

Bosnia and Herzegovina : from recovery to sustainable growth.
     p.   cm. — (A World Bank country study)
   Includes bibliographical references.
   ISBN 0-8213-3922-2
   1. Bosnia and Herzegovina—Economic policy. 2. Bosnia and
Herzegovina—Economic conditions. 3. Yugoslav War, 1991–
–Reconstruction—Bosnia and Herzegovina. I. World Bank.
II. Series.
HC402.5.B665   1997
338.949742—dc21   97-3134
                                        CIP

Contents

List of Tables, Figures, and Boxes

TABLES

FIGURES

BOXES

Preface

Bosnia and Herzegovina has experienced its first year of peace and the beginnings of political, economic, and social recovery. While life is still difficult for many Bosnian families, the reconstruction effort has already borne significant fruit. Economic growth in 1996 has reached 50 percent, and unemployment, although painfully high at over 50 percent, has declined from its postwar high of 90 percent. Many schools and health clinics have reopened, and Sarajevo airport once again began limited commercial operations. Repairs to infrastructure, essential to economic revival, are underway, and commerce is picking up, with the help of donor-financed lines of credit. Finally, the establishment, in January 1997, of the Council of Ministers and the Entity governments is an important milestone on the road to a stable political future for the country.

While these successes are encouraging, the challenge in 1997 is to build up the Dayton-mandated institutions and to make the economic recovery sustainable. Bosnia and Herzegovina must grasp this opportunity to become a truly peaceful country, open to Europe and with a free market that can offer prosperity and a better life for all its citizens and ensure freedom of religious and cultural traditions.

Prosperity and creditworthiness are still a distant vision, but one that the experience of other postwar countries shows us is within reach, with strong international support and sound domestic policies. In Bosnia, there must be good cooperation between the Entities, rapid and effective institution-building, good macroeconomic management, and sustainable sector policies. The international community, in turn, must provide adequate, well-coordinated, and timely assistance on concessional terms.

While there will be ups and downs in any peace process, the fact that tangible benefits have already reached the people of Bosnia and Herzegovina gives us real hope and energy for the future. The World Bank remains committed to the task of making peace sustainable and of helping create a better and more prosperous future for all the peoples of Bosnia and Herzegovina.

Christine Wallich
Country Director
Bosnia and Herzegovina

Abstract

Peace and reconstruction in 1996 dramatically altered the landscape of Bosnia and Herzegovina (BiH) and brought many tangible benefits to its people. Sustaining and broadening the positive developments of the past year will be the key task for the country and the international community in 1997-98. This report looks at the near-term reform issues that are essential to generating employment and providing a firm institutional and policy foundation for reconstruction and sustained economic growth. Key areas of focus include policies and expenditure reforms, including institutions for macroeconomic management, bank and enterprise privatization, and pensions and the social safety net.

Policies and Institution-building for Macroeconomic Management. Bosnia must maintain its tight fiscal policy through cash-balanced budgets, in spite of the expenditure pressures arising from reconstruction, employment generation, and social policies. The currency board approach to monetary policy, mandated by the Dayton Agreement, will provide essential credibility to the cash-balanced fiscal policy, and help build confidence in the new domestic currency more rapidly. Creating the Central Bank and adopting viable budgets at all levels of the government are institutional prerequisites for macroeconomic management. Other key requirements for effective macroeconomic management include a clear assignment of expenditure responsibilities and taxes across different levels of the government; unification of customs tariffs and trade systems of the two Entities, and institution of a viable mechanism for external borrowing and debt service.

Privatization of Enterprises and Banks. The task of reconstruction and economic recovery in Bosnia and Herzegovina is too vast for the public sector to undertake alone. A key requirement for economic revival, therefore, is the transition to a private-sector dominated market economy. Simultaneous effort is needed in three critical and linked areas: (a) privatization of socially- and state-owned assets; (b) development of a supportive business environment for existing and new private firms, and (c) development of a disciplined and competitive financial sector. The Entity-level governments will play the primary role in these areas, although some coordination mechanisms for inter-Entity issues are clearly necessary.

Reforms of the Labor-market and Social Safety Net. Unemployment throughout the country is extremely high and will, in the short term, remain so in face of a growing number of demobilized soldiers and returning refugees. Public policy should focus on encouraging employment by reducing high taxes on labor, stimulating the development of small businesses, and replacing obsolete labor-market regulations which now discourage employers from hiring. In the short term, available resources are not sufficient to provide unemployment benefits and other social benefits according to the prewar benefit formula. Direct assistance to the unemployed, to the old and disabled, and to the poor will have to be targeted and coordinated across programs, so that the very limited resources are used to ensure minimum coverage to alleviate poverty among these groups. In order to do this, eligibility for benefits must be restricted, the revenue base should be broadened, and any revenue growth in the short term should be used to increase minimum levels of protection.

Acknowledgments

This report was prepared by Wei Ding and Khaled Sherif, with the support of a team of World Bank staff and consultants. Christine Wallich, Country Director for Bosnia and Herzegovina, and Michel Noël, Chief of the Country Operations Division, Central Europe Department of the World Bank, provided overall guidance on the conceptualization and organization of the Report. Rory O'Sullivan, Director of the Bank's Resident Mission in Bosnia and Herzegovina, participated in key meetings and provided valuable help to the team. Other World Bank staff and consultants who contributed significantly to the report include Sebnem Akkaya, Emily Andrews, Charles Blitzer, Michael Borish, Xavier Devictor, William Fox, April Harding, Bart Kaminski, Saumya Mitra, Robert Palacios, and Sergei Shatalov. Additional contributions were received from Pedro Rodriguez, Lorena Alcazar, George Clarke, John Crihfield, Andrew Ewing, Luke Haggarty, Stefan Kawalec, Philip Keefer, Randi Ryterman, and Kornelis Walraven. The team would also like to thank the following individuals for their invaluable comments: Andras Horvai, Monique Koning, Baelhadj Merghoub, and Mary Sheehan of the World Bank; Sweder van Wijnbergen of the London School of Economics and the University of Amsterdam, Scott Brown, Russell Krelove, and their colleagues at the IMF; Egbert Gerken, Thomas Schiller and Gary O'Callaghan of the Office of the High Representative; Allan Jensen of the European Commission Customs and Fiscal Assistance Office; Dick Sklar, the Special Representative of the President of the United States; US Treasury and USAID officials and advisors including David Lipton, Katie Buddington, Sonal Shah, Craig Buck, Jean Tesche, Michael Markels, and Thomas P. Briggs; Joly Dixon and Joan Pearce of the European Commission, and Paul Monnory and Joshua Tanaka of the EBRD. Erlinda Inglis in the World Bank was responsible for the final production of the report.

The Bank team is indebted to the many government officials and nongovernmental experts who provided invaluable help. Key ministers and officials in the State, Federation, and Republika Srpska governments who deserve special thanks include Stijepo Andrijić, Zdenko Arapović, Zlatko Barš, Enver Backović, Muhamed Begedević, Drago Bilandžija, Pero Bosnić, Maruf Burnazović, Zoran Čolić, Sead Delić, Gojko Dursun, Avdija Fetahović, Subhija Gavranović, Fadil Haverić, Šefika Hafisović, Zlatko Hurtić, Izudin Kapetanović, Mirsad Kikanović, Novak Kondić, Vinko Kondić, Božo Ljubić, Mladen Lončar, Petra Marković, Ljiljana Marjanović, Hasan Muratović, Anka Musa, Kasim Omičević, Obrad Piljak, Jadranko Prlić, Marko Pejčinović, Slaviša Raković, Radomir Šalić, Asim Šuvalija, Neven Tomić, Mesud Sabitović, Berina Selimović-Mehmedbašić, Asim Šaković, Radovan Skoko, and Hasan Zolić.

Abbreviations and Acronyms

BiH	Bosnia and Herzegovina
BHD	Bosnia and Herzegovina dinar/Bosnian dinar
DM	Deutsche Mark
CEM	Country Economic Memorandum
EBRD	European Bank for Reconstruction and Development
FRY	Federal Republic of Yugoslavia
GDP	Gross Domestic Product
IBRD	International Bank for Reconstruction and Development
IMF	International Monetary Fund
NBBH	National Bank of Bosnia and Herzegovina
NBRS	National Bank of Republika Srpska
OECD	Organization for Economic Cooperation and Development
RS	Republika Srpska
SFRY	Socialist Federal Republic of Yugoslavia
USAID	United States Agency for International Development
VAT	Value-Added Tax

Fiscal Year

January 1 - December 31

Executive Summary

Peace and reconstruction in 1996 dramatically altered the landscape of Bosnia and Herzegovina and brought many tangible benefits to its people. The improvement is particularly visible in the Federation part of Bosnia and Herzegovina. No longer are people subject to the constant hunger, cold, and darkness that threatened them for so long. Restoration of power and water supply systems and repair of transport and communication have restarted trade and production. Schools and health clinics have reopened, providing job and income opportunities for thousands of people and essential social services to the young and the elderly. In the Federation, employment increased by more than 10 percentage points, and wage levels doubled, from an average of about DM 94 in 1995 to over DM 180 in 1996. All this occurred within the short span of 12 months.

Sustaining and broadening these positive developments of the past year will be the key task for the country and the international community in 1997. The reconstruction program needs to be accelerated and expanded to all regions of Bosnia and Herzegovina. Institutional and policy foundations must be firmly laid to prepare Bosnia and Herzegovina for sustainable recovery and growth, so that it will be able to rely increasingly on its own resources and institutions to design and implement the policies required for long-term development. In 1997, greater emphasis must be placed on establishing a viable institutional structure for effective and countrywide governance, as outlined in the Dayton Agreement, and on undertaking the key structural reforms for transforming the old socialist economic structure into a new, market-based economy.

The countrywide elections in September 1996 and the establishment of the new Bosnian government in January 1997 provide a renewed opportunity for tackling these challenges on a coordinated, countrywide basis. Success in all of these endeavors will be key in sustaining and broadening reconstruction and growth in the medium term. The international community, by providing continued support for the reconstruction program and for institution-building and economic reform, can greatly facilitate the transition to sustainable growth.

This economic report focuses on the policies essential to providing a firm foundation for reconstruction and sustained economic growth in Bosnia and Herzegovina: building an institutional and policy framework for effective macroeconomic management, privatizing banks and enterprises, fostering private-sector development, and reforming the labor-market, the pension system, and social safety net. The report concludes with a discussion of Bosnia and Herzegovina's medium-term growth prospects and financing requirements.

Building a Framework for Macroeconomic Management

Macroeconomic management requires an institutional structure within which to formulate and implement appropriate policies. It also requires the adoption of consistent policies throughout the country. Key tasks include creating common institutions, as called for by the Dayton Agreement; strengthening institutions within the Entities, particularly those in the Federation; and ensuring consistent and harmonized policies between the Entities and within the Federation. The tasks are outlined below.

Establishing a framework for monetary management

Creating a new, independent Central Bank. A stable and convertible currency is the first requirement for promoting macroeconomic stability, trade, and investment. A new, independent Central Bank must be established as the sole agency for monetary policy and currency issuance in Bosnia and Herzegovina. The Dayton Agreement calls for the Central Bank to operate as a currency board for its first six years, after which the State Parliament may decide to expand the Bank's mandate and authority. As a currency board, the Central Bank will issue currency that is fully backed by hard-currency reserves and is pegged to a fixed exchange rate relative to a major foreign currency such as the deutsche mark (DM). Creating this new Central Bank is a high-priority task.

Unifying the payments system. Following the introduction of a new countrywide currency and an independent Central Bank, the next step is to move toward further unification and reform of the payments system, both between the Entities and within the Federation. A unified payments system will greatly facilitate economic integration within and between the Entities, clearing of accounts, tax payment and transfers to the proper government, budget implementation, and private-sector commercial and financial transactions.

Establishing the framework for sustainable fiscal management

Ensuring the financing of State administration. The Dayton Agreement calls for a small, efficient State government that is responsible for foreign affairs, monetary policy, customs policy, debt management, and citizenship. Unless mandated otherwise by the State Parliament, the State does not have the capacity to tax or collect customs duties on its own and is dependent on the Entities for its funding. Under the Dayton Agreement, the Federation is to finance two thirds of the State's budget and Republika Srpska one third. How the Entities will raise the money and what mechanisms they will use for transferring the funds to the State are still to be determined. Eventually, the State should have some independent sources of revenue from taxes or customs duties. Meanwhile, the 1997 State budget could be based on revenue transfers from the Entities as a transitional arrangement. Agreement on the 1997 State budget is a high-priority task.

Assigning revenue and expenditure responsibilities within the Entities. Under the framework of the Dayton Agreement, intergovernmental arrangements will be different in Republika Srpska and the Federation. The Federation's fiscal system will be decentralized, with significant taxing and spending authority devolved to the cantons (and possibly the municipalities). A more centralized approach is expected in Republika Srpska. Assignment of spending functions to the different levels of government (Entity, canton, or municipality) needs to be based on a balance between the benefits of local decision making and the higher costs of service provision by a large number of small governments.

The Entities must also decide how to assign tax revenues. Ideally, each level within the Entity should be provided with the revenues needed to finance the services for which it is responsible. Regardless of the revenue and expenditure assignments, however, imbalances between revenue and expenditure needs are bound to emerge in some cantons or municipalities and will lead to regional differences in spending levels. The Entity governments will need to consider whether and how to limit these service differentials. Greater responsibility for spending by the Entities themselves and some type of intergovernmental grant are options for reducing the imbalances, although both may be difficult to introduce given the limited political tolerance for cross-subsidies between national groups.

Reducing the size of the public sector. Public spending accounted for about 63 percent of gross domestic product (GDP) in 1996, even as significant arrears were accruing and large portions of public expenditure were being financed by donors. Reducing public expenditures, and thereby taxes, as a share of GDP would give a large boost to economic growth. Reducing overall public spending to sustainable levels as a percentage of GDP will require major cuts and rationalization in many areas of public spending, particularly in defense, subsidies, and entitlement programs. Avoiding a buildup of large administrative structures will also be important in controlling expenditures. These improvements in expenditure management will require a more systematic budgeting approach.

Addressing outstanding claims on government. Outstanding claims of citizens on government are estimated at more than DM 10 billion in the Federation alone, more than seven times 1996 tax revenues. These claims arise from frozen foreign-exchange deposits, unpaid pensions and wages, and certificates issued to former soldiers for wages not paid during the war. While there is significant pressure to settle these claims by forgiving tax obligations or compensating claimants directly, doing so would devastate government budgets, monetary policy, and ultimately macroeconomic stability. Claims should be settled using current government assets, not future government revenues. One way to do that is to exchange claims with privatization vouchers, thereby limiting the value of claims on the government to assets to be privatized.

Reforming and harmonizing tax policies. Carefully chosen tax reforms would create an environment conducive to growth and private-sector expansion. Payroll tax rates (both wage taxes and contributions) and customs and other foreign-trade tax rates are excessive by international standards. The revenue losses from lowering these rates can be offset by broadening bases for wage and income taxes, increasing excise tax rates on both domestically and foreign-produced commodities, and better enforcement to minimize evasion. Harmonization of tax rates, tax bases, and other elements of tax policy between the Entities is particularly important for promoting economic growth and integration.

Coordinating tax collection. Tax collection is currently enforced by tax offices in each municipality. The effectiveness of such a fragmented structure is questionable. For example, maintaining uniform tax bases and rates is much more difficult with decentralized administration. A centralized system is recommended for collecting major taxes, including customs, excise, corporate, personal income, and sales or value-added taxes (VAT). But since centralization is not immediately feasible, the two Entities should, for now, coordinate and harmonize tax collection efforts to avoid tax evasion and competition as much as possible.

Clarifying responsibilities for foreign borrowing and ensuring debt service

The division of responsibilities between the State and the Entities needs to be clarified by a law on external debt. All of the fiscal capacity of Bosnia and Herzegovina rests with the Entities, which have the authority to tax and collect customs duties. Yet many creditors, particularly those holding old claims, might be obliged to conduct their financial relations through State-level institutions. Borrowing arrangements, therefore, need to take into account both the fiscal arrangements in the country and the preferences of external creditors. Furthermore, to ensure normal financial relationships between Bosnia and Herzegovina and foreign creditors, clear budgetary mechanisms for debt service need to be set up for new borrowings and for the restructured old debts. Clarifying borrowing and debt-service arrangements is a high-priority task.

Unifying foreign-trade policy and tariff structures

Under the Dayton Agreement, the State is responsible for setting trade and tariff policies. Yet, the Entities still maintain separate trade and tariff policies. The State should immediately assume responsibility for trade policy and initiate a series of reforms. Major goals include establishing a common external tariff structure with low uniform rates, enacting a new foreign-trade law that lifts most restrictions on trade flows, and negotiating accession to the World Trade Organization as well as trade liberalization agreements with other trading partners. State adoption of a law on foreign trade and customs is a high-priority task.

Harmonizing customs administration. Because customs administration is the responsibility of the Entities under the Dayton Agreement, harmonizing the administrative procedures and enforcement capacity of the two Entities is needed to avoid tax evasion and arbitrage. Within the Federation, further integration of customs administration and strengthening of the Federation Customs Administration remain crucial.

Moving Toward a Market Economy

A key element of economic reform in Bosnia and Herzegovina is continuing the transition to a market economy with a vibrant private sector. Experience in Central Europe has shown that progress requires simultaneous effort in three critical areas: developing a supportive business environment, privatizing socially- and State-owned assets, and developing a disciplined and competitive financial sector.

Improving the business environment for private enterprise

Bosnia and Herzegovina shares with the other former Yugoslav republics the institutional legacy of heavy government control of economic activity, embedded in the legal and regulatory framework. Administrative control over the economy and property expanded even further during the war, and nationalization, expropriation, and centralization occurred throughout Bosnia and Herzegovina. Still, limited private-sector activities have always been permitted, and many of the legal and institutional ingredients for private enterprise are in place, including a workable commercial code.

The Entities have already begun to revise this framework, introducing new property, competition, mortgage, and labor laws. This work needs to be completed and enforcement of the new legal framework should be underpinned by a strong and independent legal infrastructure. In addition, the governments in the Entities need to establish regular dialogue with private business people. This will send the signal that government considers the interests and needs of the private sector to be a policy priority. An open dialogue will help to establish a level playing field by alleviating concerns that powerful political interests can obtain special treatment or financing.

Privatizing socially- and State-owned enterprises

Privatization requires preparing and enacting laws regulating and mandating privatization, including the methods to be used and the means of payment. It also requires setting up an agency with full responsibility for effecting privatization.

Privatization in the Federation. Preparations for privatization have been moving ahead in the Federation under the guidance of the government-appointed privatization team. Most of the basic concepts have been agreed on and embodied in law: the Privatization Agency Law, the Law on the Privatization of Enterprises, the Law on Restitution, the Law on the Sale of Apartments with Tenant's Right of Tenure, the Law on Privatization of Banks, and the Law on the Opening Balance Sheet of Banks and Enterprises. The Privatization Agency Law has been adopted and the director and deputy director of the Federation Privatization Agency were appointed by the new Federation government in January 1997. The other five laws are at the top of the agenda of the new Federation Parliament.

Once the Federation Privatization Agency is up and running, cantonal privatization agencies will be established to handle privatization transactions within individual cantons. The Federation Agency will provide oversight and guidance and will have additional implementation responsibility for privatization transactions that involve more than one canton. Citizens will receive compensation certificates that can be used to bid on assets that are being privatized. These certificates will be related to four kinds of claims on the State: claims related to frozen foreign-exchange deposits, validated restitution claims that cannot be settled by restitution of the actual property, claims related to unpaid salaries during the war, and a general claim available to all citizens and similar to the universal vouchers used in other transition economies. The actual amounts of these claims will not be set until the legislation is passed.

Privatization in Republika Srpska. Republika Srpska passed its Law on the Privatization of Enterprises in June 1996. The basic approach envisaged is to distribute or sell shares to seven social funds (55 percent), to citizens through general vouchers (30 percent) and, where possible, to strategic investors (15 percent). Strategic investment would be achieved through public auction or a negotiated tender process that includes conditions on business activities, investments, employment, and other details.

The Republika Srpska scheme needs to be revisited. The 15 percent stake will not give a strategic investor a strong enough motive to do what is best for the company, given all the other free-riding owners. These other owners are either too passive (the social funds) or too small to undertake serious corporate governance. Conditional tenders are another problem. Other countries that have tried them have found them to be unnecessarily restrictive, unenforceable, and nontransparent. Provisions for the privatization of the social funds should be quickly and clearly outlined. Once privatized, the funds should be allowed to concentrate their ownership in specific enterprises, so they will have both the incentive and the capacity to control management. At a minimum, funds should be given clear rights to information and to vote on key company decisions. It is also critical that the framework for privatization support foreign investment, which can bring in financial resources, access to markets and current technology, and managerial know-how.

Resolving policy issues in privatization

While preparations for privatization are under way, there are still several policy issues to be resolved. Privatization needs to be accomplished quickly, so speed is of the essence. Most critical are:

- *Coordination between Entities.* Outstanding cross-border claims of enterprises, or the property claims of citizens who have moved across the inter-Entity boundary line, need to be dealt with in a coordinated fashion. The Federation and Republika Srpska must establish a workable framework for discussing these issues and coordinating the operation and privatization of infrastructure. However, resolving these outstanding claims should not become a barrier to rapid privatization of productive assets.

- *Restructuring and privatization of large industrial conglomerates will be a key challenge.* There are approximately a dozen large conglomerates in Bosnia and Herzegovina. Most of them were heavily damaged during the conflict, and some have been broken into constituent enterprises. Prewar productivity of these firms was some 40-60 percent of productivity relative to Western European competitors. These firms relied on cheap labor and large-scale subsidies to compensate for their inefficiency. It is generally neither feasible nor desirable to reconstitute them to their original structures. However, in some cases, it might be feasible to initiate some up-front organizational restructuring of some constituent enterprises when that would facilitate restarting production and exports and eventual privatization. In most cases, though, privatization of constituent enterprises need not be delayed, since future relationships between most of the constituent parts of the conglomerates would be based on commercial and contractual terms rather than on common ownership. Government should avoid the temptation to spend scarce financial resources on the large conglomerates unless private capital shows a willingness to invest.

Developing a viable financial sector

In both Entities, the banking system is burdened by the legal, regulatory, and ownership structures of the former Yugoslavia, the financial consequences of hyperinflation and imprudent lending, and damages from the war period. Most of the country's 17 socially-owned banks are in weak financial condition, with many nonperforming and unrecoverable assets, and foreign-currency denominated liabilities that cannot be serviced or repaid. The 35 private banks are small, inexperienced, and incapable of meeting the deposit and lending needs for economic recovery.

Additional institutional factors also prevent the banking sector from meeting the intermediation needs of the economy. Banks remain closely held in both Entities, and incentives still encourage lending to their enterprise shareholders. Depositors have no confidence in banks' safety and soundness. Accounting standards do not accurately reflect balance-sheet values and income and loss streams because the loan classification standards, provisioning requirements, and other regulatory guidelines needed for market-based banking are absent. Laws and court procedures to protect property rights and provide incentives to banks to lend on a secured basis are not consistent with market requirements. Prudential regulations and supervisory institutions do not yet provide the needed underpinnings for proper licensing, inspection, and bank resolution. On the demand side, lax banking practices failed to ensure debt servicing and sustainable borrowing practices on the part of enterprises.

To effectively support a market economy, the banking sector of Bosnia and Herzegovina needs to be reformed by restructuring and privatizing socially-owned banks, supporting new private banks, and strengthening the legal framework, prudential regulations, and institutional capacity for safe and sound banking.

Restructuring and privatizing socially-owned banks. Restructuring will involve severing enterprise ownership ties with insolvent banks and cleaning up troubled bank balance sheets, including the transfer of nonperforming assets, frozen foreign-currency deposits, and other foreign-currency liabilities to a separate government agency. Privatization strategies could include attracting strategic investments from domestic and foreign sources, merging restructured banks with other banks, and liquidating nonviable institutions. International investment banks could be recruited to assist in this effort.

Supporting new private banks. Some 35 private banks have opened in Bosnia and Herzegovina in recent years. Most are small, with less than DM 2.5 million in net capital, and have limited experience. Many of these banks have generated strong fee income from transfers and remittances, trade finance, and other off-balance-sheet activities. Although these activities are not sufficient to develop the country's economy, many banks now possess the building blocks for future development and growth. Further, they are unburdened by the legacy of loan problems to which the socially-owned banks in both Entities are heir.

Given the large number of these small banks, some consolidation will be inevitable and should be encouraged through appropriate banking regulations. Donor-financed technical assistance could also be used to strengthen the policies, procedures, management, and systems of viable private and socially-owned banks. Provided adequate supervision and controls would be in place, line of credit resources could also be used.

Improving the legal, regulatory, and institutional environment. Improvements in the legal, regulatory, and institutional environment are essential to developing a market-based banking system and a competitive economy. These improvements include legislation establishing the State Central Bank and Entity banking supervision agencies and laying out commercial banking guidelines in both Entities. New legislation is also required to address weaknesses in both Entities' collateral, mortgage, bankruptcy, insurance, and capital market laws. A safe and sound banking system will require new rules on connected lending, related-party lending, loan classification, loan concentration, and exposure limits on a consolidated basis; limits on enterprise ownership of banks are especially important. A new accounting framework will need to be introduced in concert with new regulations to generate the more meaningful financial information necessary for bank supervision and financial disclosure for shareholders, depositors, and borrowers.

Creating a Viable Approach to Social Assistance

The two key elements of a sustainable social assistance program are a well-functioning labor market and a sound and affordable social safety net.

Promoting employment by reforming the labor market

The growth of employment and earnings is an absolute priority for a sustainable peace in Bosnia and Herzegovina. In recent months, Entity governments have done much to encourage employment, by increasing public-service employment and developing small business opportunities. But much more can be done to improve labor markets. Employment growth is still impeded by restrictive labor laws that artificially drive up the cost of labor and by a work force whose skills are incompatible with those in demand in the labor market. Several reforms are required to support the development of a buoyant labor market:

- Payroll and wage taxes have to be reduced, to bring them in line with international standards. Overall payroll taxes have to be lowered, while contributions to pension, health, and unemployment insurance are protected. The payroll tax base needs to be broadened to bring all employers and employees, private and public, into the payroll tax net.

- Labor contracts need to be made simpler and employment practices less restrictive. Restrictions on labor contracts limit the flexibility of employment relationships and drive private employers to avoid legal contracts. Among the restrictions that need to be loosened are inflexible or expensive procedures for hiring and firing workers, overly generous provision for vacations and other types of leave, high and arbitrarily fixed minimum wages, labor-management relations based on a socialist-style collective bargaining contract, and insufficient training in the skills required in a market-oriented economy (marketing, financial planning, accounting, for example).

Providing a sustainable social safety net

Although the social needs in Bosnia and Herzegovina are tremendously high, current government commitments for pensions and health care vastly exceed the resources available. Each Entity must develop a strategy to target benefits to the most needy, providing a minimum level of income that can be financed out of the budget without excessively high or distortionary taxation.

Overhaul of pension finance. The pension system was financially unsustainable even before the war because of the rising ratio of pensioners to workers and unaffordably high benefits. Its collapse accelerated with the sudden decline in the number of contributors and earnings after 1991. The pension arrangements that survive today will not be able to provide an adequate minimum benefit for several years to come. At the same time, the payroll tax rates earmarked for pensions cannot be raised and should even be reduced if possible. In the short term, the tax base should be broadened, and any revenue growth should be used to increase minimum pensions and alleviate poverty among the old and disabled. Pension eligibility through early retirement or disability should be restricted so as to increase resources available for targeting the needy. Serious consideration should be given to a Federation-wide pension scheme and harmonization across the two Entities. This would reduce risks by expanding the pool of insured persons, reduce administrative costs, and allow for greater labor mobility.

Health care financing and insurance. Each Entity needs to reduce the near-total reliance on donor aid and to fund an affordable health insurance system that provides a basic package of essential care services. Both Entities need to find immediate sources of financing, to determine future financing arrangements, and to normalize health care. To keep tax rates low enough to facilitate employment growth, benefits need to be strictly targeted. The Federation faces the specific problem of ensuring that vast inequities do not develop between cantons, since basic health care is a canton-based responsibility under the Dayton framework.

Poverty programs. The needs of the poor are enormous throughout Bosnia and Herzegovina. Yet, there is little capacity for budgetary financing of a program of cash transfers at this time. Emergency relief, especially donations of food, which has sustained most of the population in recent years, will soon end. Consequently, a general review of social welfare programs should be undertaken to determine how best to use budgetary and donor funds and whether social programs are affordable and narrowly targeted for the poor. A poverty assessment should be undertaken quickly to help evaluate the efficacy of current welfare expenditures and to develop a plan for the future.

Rebuilding Essential Physical Infrastructure

Transportation, power, and communications infrastructure was devastated by the war and substantial resources are needed to rehabilitate it. Financial, legal, and other institutional reforms are also needed. The prices of public services must reflect their costs, and actual and implicit subsidies (in the form of nonpayment of taxes) to infrastructure sectors must be reduced. Support can be offered to the poorest users through lifeline pricing. To maximize the usefulness and operating efficiency of power, communications, and transport networks that cross Entity lines, inter-Entity coordination must be increased. Accounting and management standards require a major overhaul. In the longer term, ownership reform is needed to attract inflows of private investment to fuel development of the sector.

Normalizing External Flows Over the Medium Term

The reconstruction program that is being financed by the international community has given a tremendous boost to the economy, which increased by 50 percent in 1996. Initiation of the reconstruction program in Republika Srpska is expected to contribute to rapid economic recovery in 1997. However, this outcome will depend critically on a deepening of economic reform, strengthening of institutional capacity, continuation of financial and technical assistance from donors and, of course, perseverance in the peace process. Only then will the economic recovery be strong enough for Bosnia and Herzegovina to regain two thirds of its prewar GDP by 2000. Another three to four years will be needed to regain the prewar level of GDP.

Considerable external financing is needed to normalize Bosnia and Herzegovina's relations with international creditors, in addition to what is needed to cover reconstruction financing requirements. A strategy to resolve the debt problem should involve immediate relief in debt-service obligations (flow relief), and a permanent reduction in total indebtedness (debt-stock relief). Flow relief from external donors is particularly important to ensure a positive net transfer into the country during the recovery and to reduce debt service to a reasonable level. But for the country to return to creditworthy status and improve its chances of attracting enough private capital to replace official aid, up-front debt stock reduction is essential.

The Vision

Bosnia and Herzegovina is at a critical juncture on its road to enduring peace and sustainable reconstruction and growth. In this undertaking, people of Bosnia and Herzegovina will have to shoulder increasing responsibility in developing appropriate institutions and policies and, above all, ensuring cooperation between and within the Entities. But the international community can help to make this possible by providing continued strong support for the reconstruction program, by assisting with institution building and fundamental economic reform, and by providing significant and timely debt relief. With strong domestic reforms and consistent and timely international support, the vision of a peaceful and prosperous future for the people of Bosnia and Herzegovina is within reach.

Part One

Building a Framework for Macroeconomic Management

Although the process of establishing policies and institutions for effective macroeconomic management in Bosnia and Herzegovina was initiated in 1996, efforts focused on reconstructing essential physical infrastructure. Sustainable long-term economic growth, however, requires establishing a stable macroeconomic environment that is underpinned by effective institutions. To that end, it will be crucial for Bosnia and Herzegovina authorities to establish an integrated institutional and policy framework for managing monetary policy, collecting taxes and controlling expenditures, managing debt, and regulating trade and tariffs. In 1997 macroeconomic management efforts should focus on developing the basic institutional infrastructure for economic management and completing major liberalization programs.

In the area of monetary management, the currency-board approach to monetary policy mandated by the Dayton Agreement will provide essential credibility to fiscal policy and help build confidence in the new domestic currency. Although the Dayton Agreement does not cover bank supervision, an effective bank supervision system must be established early on to provide a sound basis for monetary management and banking-sector development. Similarly, integrating the payments system into the banking system should be an integral part of the effort.

In the area of fiscal management, urgent policy measures are required to provide a solid foundation for the emerging institutional and macroeconomic structures. These include agreements on financing for the State; coordinated revenue and expenditure reforms in both Entities, including efforts to simplify taxes, lower labor and trade taxes, and broaden the tax base; better prioritization and control over government expenditures, particularly in the areas of defense, social obligations, and administration; and restricting the settlement of domestic claims to government assets to be privatized. Entities are expected to devolve considerable fiscal responsibilities to local governments—to cantonal and municipal governments in the Federation, and municipal governments in Republika Srpska. The service delivery functions that are assigned to each level of government should balance the desire for local decision making with recognition of the higher costs that can result from service delivery by small governments. Similarly, the assignment of tax revenues to different levels of government can generate inequity because of differing abilities to finance local public services. Greater responsibility for service delivery at the Entity level or some type of intergovernmental grants formula could help reduce the imbalance, although these may be difficult to introduce given the low political tolerance for cross-subsidies between national groups.

In the area of external debt management, clearly defined rules are especially important for contracting new borrowings and for restructuring external debt, most of which is legally the responsibility of the State government.

In the area of trade and tariff regulation, two liberalization steps are essential. First, a common external tariff structure with nearly uniform rates—averaging about 8 percent, without exemptions—should be established. Second, a new foreign-trade law must be enacted that drastically limits restrictions on trade in both Entities. Both steps should be taken now, before recovery, instead of waiting to liberalize gradually as industrial output increases.

Chapter I

Recent Developments and Challenges for Macroeconomic Management

The War Brought Near-Total Economic Collapse: 1992-95

Bosnia and Herzegovina's declaration of independence at the end of 1991 was followed almost immediately by three and a half years of civil war. The war shattered the economy and devastated human and physical resources. About 200,000 people are dead or missing. More than 1 million people left the country and are scattered throughout the world. The country now has a net population of about 3.4 million people—23 percent smaller than in 1991. And about 1.5 million people are living in camps and other nonpermanent shelters.

By 1995, GDP had shrunk to less than a third of its prewar level, to about US$2.1 billion, and per capita GDP had fallen to US$500 (Table 1.1). Economic activities were almost at a standstill; industrial production had dropped more than 90 percent. Employment losses were huge, and few of the 1.3 million workers employed before the war were still employed when the war ended; at the end of 1996 unemployment remained at about 45 percent. For those who did have jobs, wages and salaries were extremely low (5-20 deutsche marks a month), and often were delayed or not paid at all. Most of the population relied on humanitarian assistance to survive. Not since World War II has a country in Central and Eastern Europe experienced such a massive economic collapse.[1]

The war's destruction of physical capital caused much of this decline. Housing units, transport and telecommunication lines and facilities, and power generation and distribution networks are in need of urgent repair and reconstruction. Government authorities estimate overall damages from the war at US$50-70 billion, and estimates of destroyed productive capacity range from US$15-US$20 billion.[2] Indirect damage due to lack of maintenance accounts for many more billions of dollars in lost productive capacity.

The war contributed to economic decline in other ways as well. It halted the economic reforms that were initiated in the former Yugoslavia before the conflict began. In addition, it divided many companies that previously had branches throughout the country. It also disrupted

---

[1] By contrast, the most severely afflicted transition economies have exhibited cumulative GDP declines on the order of 30 percent (Bulgaria, Romania, Slovakia), 40 percent (Albania, FYR Macedonia), and 50 percent (the former Soviet Union).

[2] Bosnia and Herzegovina had a GDP of US$8-9 billion before the war. Assuming a capital-output ratio of 4 to 5, the total prewar capital stock was US$30-40 billion. Since nearly half of the capital stock is estimated to have been destroyed, the damage is presumed in the range of US$15-20 billion. The government's estimates of war damages include not only physical destruction, but also the capitalized value of unpaid wage and pension arrears (such as frozen foreign-exchange deposits lost to citizens and enterprises during the war).

or eliminated previous trade and supply channels, depriving firms of markets and access to inputs (Box 1.1).

By 1994, export production had halted, and imports were confined to humanitarian in-kind assistance or goods financed by foreign aid, remittances, and local spending by foreigners. During the war, Bosnia and Herzegovina accumulated substantial arrears to international creditors; by the end of 1995, those were estimated to have reached about US$2 billion, or about 60 percent of total external debt.

During the war, separate economic management systems developed. Republika Srpska adopted the Federal Republic of Yugoslavia (FRY) dinar as well as its tax, trade, and banking legislation and procedures. In different regions in the Federation, fiscal and financial policies and management were implemented by separate authorities. In the Bosniac-majority areas, the legislation and procedures of the then Republic of Bosnia-Herzegovina continued to be applied the republic's institutions were used for enforcement. The new Bosnian dinar (BHD) was introduced as legal tender by the National Bank of Bosnia and Herzegovina (NBBH) in mid-1994. In the Croat-majority areas, new legis-lation and procedures

Table 1.1 Main Economic Indicators: Pre-Dayton [1]			
	1991	**1994**	**1995**
GDP (US$ million)	8,670	1,538	2,105
Real GDP growth (%)	..	..	33
Per capita income (US$)	1,979	357	501
Nonagricultural unemployment rate [2]			
Federation	27	..	53
Republika Srpska	27	..	53
Average Monthly Net Wages (DM) [2]			
Federation	666	..	94
Republika Srpska	666	..	51
CPI, % change, (end year) [2]			
Federation	114	780	-12
Republika Srpska	114	1,061	133
Broad Money (M2 in DM, % change)			
Federation	..	..	33
Money	..	..	45
Quasi-money	..	..	-12
Republika Srpska	..	..	-24
Money	..	..	-21
Quasi-money	..	..	-25
Fiscal Balance (cash, in DM million) [3]			
Federation (-:deficit)	..	-29	0
Revenues and grants	..	401	854
Expenditures	..	429	854
Republika Srpska (-:deficit)	..	-37	-9
Revenues and grants	..	211	188
Expenditures	..	248	197
External Current Account (in % of GDP)			
Exports of goods & non-financial services	24	9	15
Imports of goods & non-financial services	-19	-48	-63
Current Account Balance (-:deficit)	..	-8	-9
Gross Official Reserves			
in US$ millions	..	38	159
in months of imports	..	0.4	1.4
External Debt (US$ million) [4]	1,057	3,245	3,518
Debt Service Ratio (%) [5]	..	196	135

Source: National Statistical Institute, National Bank of BiH, Ministries of Finance and World Bank and IMF staff estimates.

1/ Data refer to estimates for all Bosnia and Herzegovina, unless otherwise stated.

2/ 1991 data for all Bosnia and Herzegovina.

3/ Excludes local and district government operations. Some military expenditure and associated grant financing is also excluded due to lack of data.

4/ Of the total debt stock, 50% in 1994 and 60% in 1995 is accumulated arrears.

5/ Figures refer to scheduled debt service.

based on Republic of Croatia legislation were adopted in certain cases, while in other cases legislation and procedures of the then Republic of Bosnia-Herzegovina continued to be used. The Croatian kuna was declared legal tender. But, even in cases where the two areas used the same legislation and procedures, implementation was the responsibility of separate Croat and Bosniac authorities.

Box 1.1 Bosnia and Herzegovina's Prewar Economy

Bosnia and Herzegovina was one of the lower income republics of the former Socialist Federal Republic of Yugoslavia (SFRY). Its GDP in 1990 was estimated at US$10.6 billion, or around US$1,980 per capita--considerably below the US$6,500 of Slovenia, economically the most developed republic of the former SFRY, but more than FYR Macedonia's US$1,400, economically the least developed republic of the former SFRY. It had a highly educated labor force, and more than half of its export products were sold to Western markets for hard currencies.

The economy was fairly diversified, with a large industrial base and a capable entrepreneurial class that produced complex goods such as aircraft and machine tools. About half of the output and employment was generated by large-scale industry, concentrated primarily in the energy and raw material producing sectors (especially electricity generation, wood production, coal and bauxite mining, and coke production), as well as textiles, leather, footwear, and machinery and electrical equipment. In the service sector, Bosnia and Herzegovina developed a strong capacity in civil engineering. Almost 500 engineering and construction companies operated out of Bosnia and Herzegovina before the war, generating roughly 7 percent of GDP. Agricultural production and food processing contributed less than 10 percent of GDP.

Unlike other centrally planned economies, the economic system of the former Yugoslavia was based on market socialism and self-management. Enterprises were socially owned, endowed with assets owned by society at large (there was no state-owned property) and formally run by workers' councils. In principle, key enterprise decisions were made by workers. In practice, however, decision-making was in the hands of management, which was formally selected by workers' councils and tacitly confirmed by the political system. The system was decentralized, allowing some competition in the product market, but generally restricting competition and mobility in the labor and financial markets. Commercial banks were the only source of institutional capital, and bank credit was the only form of financing for enterprises. In a system peculiar to the former Yugoslavia, banks were owned by enterprises and controlled by large enterprises, both as owners and debtors, who used banks to obtain financing on favorable terms.

Price stability in the Croat-majority areas of the Federation was achieved with the successful implementation of a stabilization program that began at the end of 1993. In August 1994, the authorities in the Bosniac-majority areas also adopted a successful stabilization program, ending hyperinflation.[3] Stabilization was facilitated by the cessation of hostilities between the communities in the Federation and rested on tight fiscal policies requiring balanced cash budgets and limiting short-term access to central-bank financing. Domestic credit, including credit to the government authorities, declined considerably.

---

[3] In August 1994 the NBBH introduced currency reform, redenominating the Bosnian dinar and restricting the status of legal tender to the new Bosnian dinar and, for some transactions, the deutsche mark. The new dinar was viewed as a transitional currency until peace and economic stability were restored. The dinar is pegged to the deutsche mark at a fixed exchange rate of 100 to 1. To support this fixed exchange rate policy, the central government adopted a policy of balancing the budget on a cash basis, requiring no financing from the NBBH. Since the second half of 1994, the NBBH has limited the expansion of base money to whatever purchases of foreign exchange it could effect in the market, a strategy that successfully stabilized the currency.

With stabilization, the retail price index in the Federation fell by 12 percent in 1995. Despite a large increase in the price index of domestic services, the prices of traded goods sharply declined. Production indicators in most economic subsectors increased by 200-600 percent in 1995 relative to 1994. With the resumption of economic activity and inflows of foreign aid, the National Bank of Bosnia and Herzegovina's net foreign asset position improved somewhat. Backed largely by these reserves, money in circulation increased, reflecting the public's increased confidence in the Bosnian dinar and the revival of economic activity in the Bosniac-majority areas. Together with an increase in demand deposits by enterprises and public institutions in Croat-majority areas, this caused the broad money supply to expand in 1995.

In Republika Srpska, the economic situation started to improve in early 1994, when the Federal Republic of Yugoslavia adopted a stabilization program involving a fixed exchange-rate policy and strict supporting policies (known as the Avramović plan). In August 1994, however, Republika Srpska's economy suffered a major setback when Federal Republic of Yugoslavia joined other nations in imposing sanctions mandated by the United Nations. These sanctions included an embargo on external trade, a cutoff of telecommunications, the freezing of Republika Srpska's financial accounts and assets held in the Federal Republic of Yugoslavia, and tight restrictions on border crossings. Republika Srpska responded by tightening controls on spending, raising tax rates and improving collections, and directing credit and supplies to maintain a minimum of domestic production. Output declined significantly and prices rose. Because direct domestic and external borrowing were not available, fiscal accounts were balanced on a cash basis, although there was a substantial accumulation of arrears.

Initiation of Reconstruction Program Started Economic Recovery: 1996

The Dayton Agreement and implementation of a major donor assistance program in 1996 set the stage for economic recovery, especially in the Federation.[4] This recovery was facilitated by continued adherence to the stabilization policies of 1994. Membership in the international financial institutions—the International Monetary Fund (IMF), World Bank, and the European Bank for Reconstruction and Development (EBRD)—also helped by normalizing Bosnia and Herzegovina's financial relations with the outside world. These institutions helped Bosnia and Herzegovina to develop an economic policy framework under which the international assistance was provided. The framework encouraged maintenance of macroeconomic stability by continuing to limit the fiscal deficit of the consolidated public sector to levels compatible with available sources of foreign financing.

---

[4] The donor assistance program provides across-the-board financial and technical support to ensure sustainable employment creation and growth. The program's goals include preventing bottlenecks in all areas of infrastructure and providing basic services in health, education and housing; ensuring minimal living standards for the most vulnerable segments of the population; and rapidly establishing institutions for economic management, with an emphasis on the development of a private sector and the transition to a market economy.

Strong recovery in the Federation

Industrial production in the Federation increased almost 90 percent during the first eleven months of 1996 over the same period in 1995, reflecting increased production of wood products, textiles and apparel, and foodstuff and beverages (Table 1.2). Because it started from a very low base, however, production in the second half of 1996 was still just 10 percent of its prewar level. Most prewar conglomerates remained idle in the absence of a clear restructuring and privatization strategy, discouraging foreign investors and delaying donor assistance. Private enterprises and small- and medium-sized firms, on the other hand, were becoming very active, mostly in services such as trade and transport. Recovery was most noticeable in the Bosniac-majority areas, reflecting the limited production base before the recovery started and the large scale of international assistance. Production and trade also improved in the Croat-majority areas, but the rate of increase was more moderate, reflecting a much less depressed level of production before 1996. Exports also increased, mainly in wood products.

Table 1.2 Economic Trends in the Federation, 1996	
	1996
Industrial Production	
% change, Jan.-Nov. 96/Jan.-Nov. 95	87
Nonagricultural unemployment rate (%)	44
Average Monthly Net Wages (DM) [1]	182
Average Monthly Pensions (DM) [1]	65
CPI, (% change over end-95)	3
Broad Money (M2, % change over end-95) [1] [2]	110
Money	237
Currency in circulation [3]	285
Demand deposits	203
Quasi-money [4]	89
Fiscal Balance (cash, in DM million)	-5
1/ Data refer to Jan.-Nov. period.	
2/ Defined as currency (BHD) in circulation, plus demand	
deposits and time and savings deposits (in BHD) and	
foreign currencies).	
3/ Excluding foreign currency.	
4/ Time and savings deposits.	
Source: National Statistical Institute, National Bank of BiH, Ministry of Finance, World Bank, and IMF Staff estimates.	

The increase in economic activity has had notable employment effects. In the Federation, nonagricultural unemployment at the end of 1996 was about 10 percentage points lower than at the end of 1995. Unemployment remained extremely high, however, at about 45 percent. Net monthly wages (after wage taxes and social contributions) doubled from their levels at the end of the war, averaging about DM 180 in 1996. Pension payments resumed in the Bosniac-majority areas in early 1996, with the average monthly payment reaching DM 65, a level comparable to that paid in the Croat-majority areas, but still far below prewar levels. Prices remained broadly stable throughout the year.

The authorities in the Federation have been able to sustain financial stability, albeit with continued accumulation of arrears During 1996, the cash budget balance was maintained despite the increase in public sector wages. This achievement was due to significant improvements in tax collection, particularly in sales, custom, and excise taxes, and to fiscal support from donors (for details of fiscal developments in 1996, see Chapter III). The monetary policies of the NBBH continued to be based on currency board principles—restricting emissions of the Bosnian dinar to hard currency holdings or relying on foreign currencies (DM and kuna). Gross official international reserves increased significantly, reflecting disbursements of external assistance, as did (though to a lesser extent) inflows to the domestic private sector from Bosnian residents abroad. There was a corresponding increase in broad money, driven largely by a sharp increase in the dinars in circulation and in the demand deposits of the private sector.

A slower start in Republika Srpska

Recovery in Republika Srpska began only after international sanctions were lifted in March 1996, and has proceeded at a slower pace than in the Federation. Although trade and the supply of basic commodities improved and consumer prices fell 9 percent during 1996 (Table 1.3), basic constraints to supply and production, particularly in nonagricultural sectors, remain largely unchanged. In late 1996, production was eight to 10 percent of its prewar level. Nonagricultural unemployment is estimated to have exceeded 60 percent in 1996. Wage and income levels were still low at the end of 1996, with monthly net average wages of about DM 60. Pension payments were even lower, averaging DM 33 a month.

Table 1.3 Economic Trends in Republika Srpska, 1996	
	1996
Industrial Production	
% change, Oct. 96/Dec. 95	58
Nonagricultural unemployment rate (%)	61
Average Monthly Net Wages (DM) [1]	61
Average Monthly Pensions (DM) [1]	33
CPI, (% change over end-95)	-9
Broad Money (M2, % change over end-95) [1][2]	-2
Money (excluding foreign currencies)	-100
Quasi-money	14
Fiscal Balance (cash, in DM million)	-1
1/ Data refer to Jan.-Nov. period.	
2/ Defined as demand deposits plus time and savings deposits in Yugoslav dinar and other foreign currencies.	
Source: Ministry of Finance of Republika Srpska, World Bank, and IMF Staff estimates.	

Future Efforts Should Focus on Building Common Institutions and Sustainable Policies

Although efforts to establish the economic policies and institutions called for in the Dayton Agreement began in 1996, progress has been limited. At the State level, common institutions (such as a new Central Bank) and policies (such as customs and trade policies) have not been established. The country remains economically divided. In the Federation, other key areas of economic management—including tax policies and administration, budget and banking systems, and pension and health finance—are still largely uncoordinated.

Fragmentation in institutional structure and policies presents major risks to recovery, reconstruction, and macroeconomic stability. In 1997, Bosnia and Herzegovina must develop an institutional and governance framework for monetary management, fiscal management, external borrowing and debt management, and trade and customs administration if peace and reconstruction are to be sustained. Resolving these issues will require political compromise among all three parties in Bosnia and Herzegovina. Although the Dayton Agreement provides an outline for addressing some of these issues, many details have yet to be worked out. The chapters that follow analyze the issues involved and recommend practical solutions.

Chapter II

Monetary Institutions and Policies for Postwar Stability

Monetary management in Bosnia and Herzegovina is complicated by the de facto division of the country into three monetary areas: the Bosnian dinar-based Bosniac-majority area, the kuna-based Croat-majority area (both in the Federation), and the FRY dinar-based Republika Srpska. The National Bank of Bosnia and Herzegovina manages the money supply in the Bosniac-majority area. On December 5, 1996, the NBBH announced that the Bosnian dinar was convertible for current-account transactions. There is no exclusive monetary authority in the Croat-majority area since it is effectively part of the Croatian kuna area. The kuna is convertible for current account transactions. In Republika Srpska, the National Bank of Republika Srpska (NBRS) performs only limited monetary authority functions since Republika Srpska uses the Yugoslav dinar as its legal tender and does not have its own currency. The Yugoslav dinar is not convertible. In the Federation, the newly created Federation Banking Agency is responsible for bank licensing and supervision, while in Republika Srpska the National Bank performs official bank regulatory and supervisory functions.

The New Central Bank Will Function as a Currency Board

Bosnia and Herzegovina's Constitution, formally ratified in early 1996, mandates that a new independent Central Bank be established as the sole agency responsible for setting monetary policy and issuing currency for the entire country. The Central Bank's four-member governing board, including the governor, was appointed by the newly elected presidency in December 1996. To enhance the Central Bank's chances of survival and to insulate it from political influence, its governor for the first six years is recommended to the State's presidency by the IMF. The governor cannot be a citizen of Bosnia and Herzegovina or of any of its neighboring states. The three remaining board members are a Bosniac and a Bosnian Croat—both representing the Federation—and a representative of Republika Srpska. The two members of the Federation share one vote on the board, the member from Republika Srpska has one vote, and the governor casts the third and tie-breaking vote.

For the first six years following its inception, the Central Bank is required to function as a currency board. The currency board will maintain a fixed exchange rate relative to a hard currency, which is expected to be the deutsche mark. In order to maintain the fixed exchange rate, issues of local currency must closely track the Central Bank's holdings of hard currency reserves. Thus, the credibility of the fixed exchange rate requires that the Central Bank's stock of international reserves should always be sufficient to ensure the convertibility of the Central Bank's liabilities (currency and bank reserves held by the Central Bank). The fixed exchange rate, together with the required stock of foreign-exchange reserves, will then ensure the credibility of the new currency. After the first six years, the State Parliament may decide to abolish the Central Bank's currency-board status and expand its mandate and authority.

The Currency-Board Arrangement Creates Several Challenges

The creation of a currency board in Bosnia and Herzegovina presents certain challenges, particularly for monetary and credit management, fiscal policy, banking-sector regulation, and exchange-rate management.

A currency board constrains monetary and credit management

The first challenge stems from the fact that the currency board will limit the authorities' flexibility in pursuing an independent monetary policy. The currency board system requires that monetary creation closely track—and not exceed—the Central Bank's hard currency holdings. Thus, monetary and credit policies are essentially excluded as instruments for jump-starting the economy and for supporting economic expansion. To the contrary, monetary policy will be somewhat restrictive if hard currency earnings and inflows grow more slowly than payments for imports and other external obligations. Still, the hyperinflation experienced in the past and the uncertainty that most investors still feel in the aftermath of the war make it essential to increase confidence in the currency through a currency board arrangement.

Fiscal policy is also constrained

A related issue is the limitation that the currency-board arrangement will impose on the conduct of fiscal policy in Bosnia and Herzegovina. Because of the Central Bank's inability under the currency board arrangement to extend credit, even to the government, fiscal policy—particularly the option of incurring fiscal deficits—will be much more constrained. Not only can the Central Bank not extend credit to the government, but other banks will have great difficulty in accommodating the government's financing needs, given that they will not be able to obtain credit from the Central Bank. Thus, a currency-board arrangement demands prudent fiscal policies and management (see Chapter III).

Managing liquidity in the banking sector is difficult

Another challenge of a currency-board arrangement relates to management of short-term liquidity problems that might arise in the banking sector. A currency board is usually unable to serve as a lender of last resort unless it holds excess reserves in sufficiently large amounts. Since Bosnia and Herzegovina is a small, open economy with essentially free capital flows, fluctuations in liquidity might be much higher than in other countries with currency-board type arrangements, leading to large variations in hard currency reserve holdings. Currency boards typically respond to increased outflows by raising domestic interest rates, in order to sustain the target exchange rate. But, unless short-term Central Bank instruments are developed, the Central Bank will have trouble influencing interest rates or liquidity in the economy.

In addition, the Central Bank will be unable to help solvent banks that might encounter temporary liquidity problems. Although this is an important issue that policymakers need to bear in mind, it might not be a significant concern in the near term. First, the overwhelming problem in the banking sector is insolvency rather than illiquidity. The appropriate response to solvency issues is to ensure that bank owners have sufficiently high equity stakes in their banks. The authorities should resist the temptation to quickly come to the rescue of the banking sector when liquidity difficulties surface, because it is often difficult for regulators to distinguish bank solvency problems from liquidity problems. Second, intervention to prevent liquidity crises is intended to avoid disruption of the financial system (that is, bank runs), with its consequent impact on activities in the real sector and a generalized collapse of real asset values. However, Bosnia and Herzegovina's financial system has relatively few links to the real economy. Credit flows are extremely low. Credit claims on the private sector are less than 15 percent of GDP, and most were extended before the war. Demand deposits held by the private sector are less than 3 percent of GDP. In industrial countries, private credit claims are usually about 100 percent of GDP and demand deposits, about 25 percent.

As the financial system grows, liquidity issues, even in the context of a currency board, can be dealt with by requiring banks to hold a significant portion of their liabilities—say, 30 percent—in the form of DM bonds. These bonds could be deposited with the Central Bank to ensure compliance with liquidity requirements, in which case they would function like a large, interest-bearing reserve requirement. A second solution is to encourage foreign bank entry into the domestic financial sector. Foreign banks could help strengthen Bosnia and Herzegovina's financial system because they are much better diversified than the domestic banks that do business only in Republika Srpska or the Federation, each a very small market. In the meantime, the need to avoid liquidity crises highlights the urgency and importance of developing an effective bank supervision framework and supervision capacity (see Chapter VII).

Exchange rate management must be disciplined and decisive

Finally, a currency board arrangement raises several issues for exchange-rate management. The objective of all currency boards is to build confidence in the domestic currency by guaranteeing the convertibility of local money into hard currency at a fixed exchange rate. But there are always many temptations to devalue, particularly to stimulate exports or to discourage capital outflows. Successful currency boards also might tempt policymakers to correct appreciation of the currency or to devalue. For example, the increased credibility that a successful currency board generates could lead to large foreign-investment inflows (mainly financed by Bosnia and Herzegovina nationals from their foreign-held assets). If the currency board monetizes these inflows, it will have inflationary effects unless the board can sterilize the inflows through the sale of bonds. The resulting inflation and real appreciation might undercut export competitiveness. Rather than working to increase their productivity, exporters might seek to restore competitiveness by devaluing or by correcting real appreciation.

Over the next six years, devaluation for any reason—including satisfying the demands of exporters—will undermine the currency board and so erode confidence in the local currency. This six-year period is not long by international standards, and Bosnia and Herzegovina will do well to have established confidence in its currency by that time. Thus, it is essential that the exchange rate not be adjusted once it has been set. These considerations point to the need for careful deliberations when the new currency is introduced and its exchange rate is set. In particular, the initial exchange rate should be set with a comfortable margin to take into account the potential pressure for appreciation, which is likely to accompany the large foreign-exchange inflows associated with Bosnia's reconstruction program. If the currency appreciates, policy corrections to assist exporters should focus on lowering the costs of business caused by government intervention—such as reducing payroll tax rates to levels more in line with world standards.

Unifying the Payments System Is Essential

Former Yugoslavia's complex system of payments bureaus continues, separately, in the two Entities. The bureaus are government-owned and government-operated clearing and settlement agencies that also perform tax collection and auditing functions unrelated to their clearing activities. In the Federation, the use of different currencies in the Bosniac- and Croat-majority areas has prevented unification of the payments system. Instead, settlement of payments between the two areas of the Federation is conducted in deutsche marks, and only periodically. In addition, the system is a monopoly and not transparent in its operations. This system deprives banks of much needed liquidity and resources for lending. It also prevents the development of a modern clearing system for payments and an efficient interbank market, institutions which are essential if the currency board system is to function smoothly with the banking system.

Unifying the payments system throughout the country would facilitate the clearing of accounts, payment of taxes, transmittal of taxes to the proper government, implementation of government budgets, and other private and commercial financial transactions. Other essential reforms include removing nonessential functions from the payments system (such as tax collection and auditing, which should be functions of the Entity tax administrations) and modernizing operations. Over the longer term, demonopolization and integration of the payments function into the banking sector will be crucial.

Chapter III

Fiscal Management and Policy

Bosnia and Herzegovina's tax base collapsed soon after the outbreak of war. Local governments collected what taxes they could to provide local services. In the initial years of the conflict, the government of the Bosniac-majority area financed about 90 percent of expenditures through credits from the NBBH, which quickly resulted in hyperinflation. In the summer of 1994, a stabilization program implemented in the Bosniac-majority areas recentralized tax collection and budget management and restored the payments system in those areas. Significant fiscal tightening also occurred in 1994 as a result of the sanctions imposed by the Federal Republic of Yugoslavia.

Limited revenue, a limitation reinforced by the monetary arrangements and discipline imposed by the NBBH, has restricted government expenditures in all jurisdictions to the only sources of financing that have been available—domestic tax revenue and foreign financing. This restriction ensured monetary and price stability, one of the most important factors underlying the economic recovery in 1995-96.

This fiscal scenario, however, is under increasing pressure. The economic recovery in 1996 was accompanied by a strong rebound in fiscal revenue; however, expenditures rose even faster. Public expenditures in 1996, including those financed by donors, might account for as much as 63 percent of GDP. While such a high level of expenditures might have been unavoidable in 1996, it is not sustainable in the medium term. It was made possible partly by the extraordinary efforts by 58 donors—47 countries and 11 organizations—that have supported about 40 percent of public expenditures (by covering recurrent government and social expenditures, public investment projects, and foreign obligations). This support will decline. To correct the long-term imbalance between revenues and expenditures, reform needs to start immediately. On the revenue side, tax reforms should ensure that adequate revenues are efficiently and effectively collected. In particular, the reliance on certain distortionary taxes, such as wage and customs taxes, should be reduced while the tax base is broadened and collection is improved. On the expenditure side, public expenditures need to be rationalized and prioritized. An additional threat to fiscal viability is the country's large stock of domestic and foreign liabilities. It will not be possible to put public finances on firm footing until these issues are addressed.

The development of a sustainable fiscal situation will take place in a complex, uncertain, and evolving institutional setting. Government structures are still developing based on the Dayton Agreement and the constitutions for the State and Entities. Within this developing framework, several institutional issues need to be resolved, including securing financing for the State administration and for external debt obligations, coordinating fiscal and tax policy between the Entities, and developing mechanisms for assigning revenues and expenditures within the Entities.

Fiscal Developments in 1996

The two most important fiscal developments in 1996 were the rapid expansion in revenues and expenditures and the modest adjustments made to the institutional structure for fiscal management.

Table 3.1 Fiscal Revenues in Bosnia and Herzegovina, 1995 and 1996 [1]

	BiH [2] Consolidated budget	BiH Consolidated budget	State budget	Federation-level budget	Canton & municipal budgets Bosniac-maj. [3] areas	Croat-maj. [3] areas	Total Federation	Republika Srpska budget
In DM Million	*1995*	-----------			--------1996-----------			---------
Tax Revenue	574	1,398	--	329	630	193	1,152	246
Sales taxes	201	544	--	--	378	107	485	59
Excise taxes	118	222	--	148	43	14	204	17
Custom duties	111	314	--	181	19	19	219	95
Wage and income taxes [4]	102	297	--	--	178	46	224	72
Other taxes	42	22	--	--	12	8	20	2
Social Security Contributions	244	519	--	--	329	127	457	62
Nontax Revenue and Grants	225	122	57	6	49	4	58	7
o/w transfer to State from Entities	--	31	31	--	--	--	--	--
Total Revenue	1,043	2,040	57	335	1,008	324	1,667	315
Share of GDP [5]								
Tax Revenue	15.5	29.0	...	...	...	...	33.0	18.0
Sales taxes	5.4	11.0	...	...	...	...	14.0	4.0
Excise taxes	3.2	5.0	...	...	...	...	6.0	1.0
Custom duties	3.0	6.0	...	...	...	...	6.0	7.0
Wage and income taxes [4]	2.8	6.0	...	...	...	...	6.0	5.0
Other taxes	1.1	0.5	...	...	...	...	1.0	0.1
			...	...	...	...		
Social Security Contributions	6.6	11.0	...	...	...	...	13.0	4.0
Nontax Revenue and Grants	6.1	3.0	...	...	...	...	1.0	1.0
Total Revenue	28.2	42.0	...	...	...	...	48.0	23.0

Source: Data provided by authorities, and Bank and IMF staff estimates.

[1] Preliminary information. Local government operations in Republika Srpska are excluded due to lack of data.
Exchange rates used: DM 1 = Kuna 3.7 = FRY Dinar 2.72 = BHD 100 = 0.67 USD; RS data do not include municipal revenue.

[2] Excludes local government and district operations.

[3] Includes operations of administrations in the process of being replaced under the Federation Agreement.

[4] Includes wage tax for reconstruction.

[5] For the first nine months of 1996, GDP is assumed to be three-fourths of estimated annual GDP.

"--" = not available; "..." = not applicable.

Revenues and expenditures expand rapidly

In 1996, tax collections were about 29 percent of GDP, or DM 1,398 million—an increase of 144 percent over 1995 and 281 percent over 1994 (Table 3.1). Including social security contributions and nontax revenues and grants, fiscal revenues totaled to DM 2,040 million in 1996, about equal to total government expenditures for 1996. Thus, public expenditures funded by the government's own resources amounted to about 42 percent of GDP in 1996. All parts of the country have operating budgets that are more or less balanced on a cash-flow basis (that is, cash expenditures are limited to the amount of fiscal revenues). In 1996, Bosnia and Herzegovina ran a DM 6 million cash deficit (Table 3.2). Military expenditures from budgetary sources accounted for less than 10 percent of the total budget; social fund expenditures and other transfer payments amounted to about one third.

Table 3.2 Fiscal Expenditures in Bosnia and Herzegovina, 1995 and 1996[1]

	BiH[2] Consolidated budget	BiH Consolidated budget	State budget	Federation-level budget	Canton & municipal budgets[3]	Total Federation	Republika Srpska budget
In DM Million	1995	-- 1996 ---					
Expenditures							
Wages and Contributions	87	222	31	50	104	153	38
Goods and Services	206	91	23	11	20	31	36
Military	374	189	...	--	50	50	139
Interest	--	12	...	--	12	12	--
Social Expenditures	217	524	...	4	458	462	62
Reconstruction Expenditures	...	17	...	3	9	12	5
Subsidies	--	36	...	29	0	29	7
Other Transfer to Households	--	392	...	178	190	369	23
Other Expenditures and Unallocated[4]	167	564	4	76	477	553	7
Total Expenditures [5]	1,051	2,046	58	351	1,320	1,672	317
Memo item:							
Budget Balance ("+"=surplus) [5]	-8	-6	-1	-16	12	-5	-1

Source: Data provided by authorities and Bank and IMF staff estimates.
1/ Preliminary data. Exchange rates used: DM1 = BHD 100 / YD 3.4 / Kuna 3.7.
2/ Excludes local government and district operations for the Republika Srpska.
3/ Includes operations of administrations in the process of being replaced under the Federation Agreement.
4/ For 1996, includes district, canton, and municipal expenditures, for which sufficient data are not available to allocate to other categories.
5/ Cash basis.
"--" = not available; "..."=not applicable.

However, significant public-sector expenditures took place outside of the budget, making actual public spending much larger; the difference was financed by donors. Disbursement of donor assistance amounted to about US$1.1 billion in 1996, about 65 - 70 percent of this amount was used for public expenditures. Thus, total public spending could be US$0.7 billion more than is shown in Table 3.2, making public-sector expenditures totaling about 63 percent of 1996 GDP, a level that is unsustainable.

Donor assistance is expected to wind down after 1998 or 1999. At the same time, the expansion of domestically generated fiscal revenue is constrained by the size and the growth rate of the economy. Under the optimistic scenario that GDP reaches US$4.5 billion in 1998, total domestically generated fiscal expenditure cannot exceed US$1.8 billion if the ratio of taxes to GDP is held to no more than 40 percent. A major adjustment of revenues and expenditures will be needed for the fiscal situation to become sustainable.

In 1996, the Federation was more successful at generating revenues than Republika Srpska. The Federation collected DM 1,152 million in tax revenues, or DM 512 per inhabitant, compared with DM 246 million in Republika Srpska, or about DM 246 per inhabitant (see Table 3.1). Estimated tax revenue in the Bosniac-majority areas totaled DM 630 million in 1996, with more than half coming from the sales tax on goods and services. Estimated revenue in the Croat-majority areas totaled DM 193 million, with additional estimated revenue from three extrabudgetary funds of DM 89 million. The sales tax was also the main source of tax revenue in the Croat-majority areas.

Total expenditures for the Federation in 1996 amounted to DM 1,672 million. In Republika Srpska, expenditures totaled DM 317 million. Wage expenditures were DM 153 million for the Federation and DM 38 million for Republika Srpska. Social expenditures (including support for health, education, and invalid and war causalities) totaled to DM 462 million in the Federation, or DM 205 per person, and DM 62 million in Republika Srpska, or DM 62 per person (see Table 3.2).

The institutional structure for fiscal management is evolving

The Federation. Because of the fighting between Bosnian Croats and Bosniacs in 1993-94, the Croat-majority areas instituted a separate fiscal system, including separate tax administration, headquartered in Mostar, and a customs administration. The Washington Agreement of April 1994 called for the tax and customs administrations in the Croat- and Bosniac-majority areas to be replaced by Federation administrations. Import regimes were harmonized in March 1995 following the Federation Assembly's adoption of a Customs and Tariff Law similar to the Croatian import regime. But, the Federation did not assume even minimal governing authority until February 1996, when the governments of the State and the Federation were officially separated. In April 1996, the customs administrations were merged into a single Federation Customs Administration that collects customs duties, special import taxes, and excise taxes on imported goods for the entire Federation.

Reform has progressed more slowly in other areas of fiscal management. A law centralizing tax administration at the Federation level was passed in June 1996, but has not yet come into effect. The Bosniac- and Croat-majority areas continue to maintain separate tax administrations and budgets. Although Federation tax legislation has been passed for sales, excise, and customs taxes, enforcement is weak. Work is still under way on corporate and personal income taxes.

Republika Srpska. Republika Srpska has a separate, centralized fiscal system. Its laws and regulations are based mostly on those of the Federal Republic of Yugoslavia. Its institutions (customs and tax administration) operate with a great degree of arbitrariness. Cooperation between the fiscal institutions of Republika Srpska and those of the Federation was nearly nonexistent in 1996.

Expenditure and Tax Policies Must Be Reformed to Achieve Sustainable Fiscal Management

Three factors threaten the goal of long-term fiscal sustainability. The first is the severe mismatch between budgetary resources and expenditure needs. The second is the government's large overhang of domestic liabilities, mainly citizens' foreign-exchange deposits in the banking sector, pensions, and back wages for soldiers. The third is the tax system's excessive reliance on payroll and trade taxes.

Limiting public expenditures for fiscal sustainability

If the growing pressures on fiscal expenditures are not addressed directly, they are certain to destabilize the macroeconomy and derail efforts to achieve fiscal sustainability. The dangers arise from large social expenditures, off-budget investment spending, the need to fully incorporate military expenditures into budgets, and the cost of administrative structures at all levels of government.

Although social and other needs are pressing, it is essential that budgets for each area remain balanced on both a cash and an accrual basis to maintain macroeconomic stability. Thus, governments must avoid resorting to arrears. Although government borrowing is curtailed under the currency-board arrangement, the temptation to borrow could grow at each level of government unless public-expenditure priorities are carefully set and the overall size of the government is clearly restrained. To that end, a public-expenditure review is now being undertaken to examine and prioritize public expenditures in Bosnia and Herzegovina.

Social expenditures

In the next few years, budgets for social needs will be under tremendous pressure. Current budget outlays are artificially low in some areas and will rise either because donor contributions cannot be sustained or because service provision will rise as schools, clinics, and hospitals resume operations. For other social welfare expenses, which are extrabudgetary in some jurisdictions, unmet needs are at least as big a problem. Moreover, even the low levels of self-funding that have been maintained have required excessive payroll tax rates in both Entities.

The health fund in Republika Srpska is extrabudgetary, but as is the case throughout Bosnia and Herzegovina emergency relief and humanitarian aid still cover most health-care costs. Republika Srpska's health fund is managed on a regional basis under a national umbrella and has been used primarily to pay staff salaries. Fund expenditures have covered about 20 percent of health-care costs; emergency aid has covered the rest. Although the health fund in the Bosniac-majority areas of the Federation was brought within the government budget, these areas also have relied on unsustainable foreign assistance for the bulk of medical care, from physicians to pharmaceuticals. Budgetary support for these health funds, and for pension funds, might be unavoidable (see Chapter IX).

Relieving the budgetary pressures created by social expenditures will require a two-pronged approach. On the revenue side, where tax rates should fall (particularly on wages), tax exemptions must be drastically curtailed so that revenue levels can be sustained through a broader tax base with fewer distortions. Some broad-based taxes, such as sales and excise taxes, can be increased somewhat. On the expenditure side, there must be significant efforts to target assistance for all social welfare spending: for example, restricting eligibility to those most in need by raising retirement ages and providing a minimal floor of protection, while setting a ceiling on benefits. Alternative mechanisms for social protection, such as private insurance, can also be considered. But even when these measures have been taken, greater budgetary resources will likely be needed to fund benefits to people who qualify for them. Such increases will have to be incorporated into future budgets, and funded by expanding the tax base.

Government investment spending

Government accounts must start reflecting the full extent of the governments' role in economic activity. In particular, the large investment program supported as part of the reconstruction program needs to be fully integrated into the Entity budgets, and shown as being foreign financed. This integration is also key to ensuring that investments generate the counterpart funds needed to maintain the infrastructure being rehabilitated. If this integration was performed retroactively for the 1996 Entity budgets, expenditures would show a rise of at least DM 550 million over the DM 2,046 million of consolidated spending shown in Table 3.2. The value of these externally-financed investments alone would increase the ratio of public expenditures to GDP by 10 percentage points in 1996—not including other recurrent public expenditures financed by donors.

Military spending

Military expenditures must be carefully reviewed and incorporated into the 1997 budget. Although the consolidated budget in 1996 shows that only about 10 percent of public expenditure was allocated to the military, substantial, nontransparent sources of financing for the military exist outside the government budget. As military expenditures are reincorporated into government budgets and the external financing dwindles, pressure on budgets is bound to rise unless the size of the military is drastically reduced. Current military spending is far greater than needed to foster an atmosphere of security. Excessive military expenditures also impede both growth and poverty reduction by diverting resources that could be better spent on infrastructure or education and by undermining macroeconomic stability. Coordination is needed to ensure that military spending is cut according to the plans laid out in the Dayton Agreement and implemented at the same time in both Entities.

Public administration

Finally, great care must be taken to avoid building large administrative structures for the governments—a very real threat given by the many governments in Bosnia and Herzegovina. Excessive staff in administrative agencies that are no longer needed under the Dayton structure should be reduced, including the separate tax administrations in the Bosniac- and Croat-majority areas of the Federation. New administrations (as in the cantons) should be extremely careful in appointing new staff and should avoid saddling local governments with too many employees. Canton, district, and municipal expenditures will account for a large portion of total public spending, so prudent resource management, including personnel management at these lower levels of government, is crucial.

Addressing domestic claims

Further complicating the efforts to restore fiscal balance are the large internal liabilities that the various governments have assumed. There are outstanding claims for up to DM 3 billion in frozen foreign-exchange deposits, DM 2 billion or more in unpaid pensions and wages, and perhaps DM 5 billion in back wages for soldiers in both Entities. These DM 10 billion in claims—more than seven times consolidated budgetary expenditures in the Federation in 1996— simply are not affordable. While other parts of the former Yugoslavia (Croatia, Slovenia, and the Federal Republic of Yugoslavia) also inherited domestic claims, these were a much smaller fraction of GDP and were potentially manageable through fiscal policy. That is not the case in

Bosnia and Herzegovina. Because there is no fiscal solution for addressing these claims, a non-fiscal policy for them must be introduced.

Besides the fact that there are no resources to satisfy these claims, Bosnia and Herzegovina is asking Paris Club and London Club lenders to accept a steep discount on debt obligations. Lenders are unlikely to respond positively if domestic claims are being created and honored at 100 percent of their face value at the same time that Bosnia and Herzegovina is claiming an inability to service foreign debt. External debt, discussed below and in Chapters IV and XI, totals about US$3.5 billion, more than US$2 billion of which is in arrears. Bosnia is asking external creditors to discount their claims generously. Even with generous debt reduction there will still be significant debt-service requirements that should be included in the government's spending plans; these should not be crowded out by Bosnia and Herzegovina's policies toward domestic claims.

Thus, it is imperative that the case-by-case recognition of claims be curtailed, and that previous decrees and laws creating these claims be repudiated. For example, former soldiers were issued bank books in which their back wages were inscribed. The canton of Sarajevo and other cantons accepted deductions from these books as payment for utilities, for the purchase of canton property, and other purposes. This approach cannot continue. Instead, settlement of domestic claims should be guided by two principles.

First, the real value of payments on the domestic claims cannot be higher than what is being offered to external creditors, as mentioned above. If external creditors are to consider deep discounts on their claims on Bosnia and Herzegovina, they must see domestic creditors accepting similar discounts. Generous payments by the government to domestic claimants will be seen by external creditors as convincing evidence that the country is capable of servicing its full external debt.

Second, domestic claims should be settled by using current government assets, not future government revenues. Given the extremely tight budgetary situation, any cash payment or its equivalent should be avoided. The budget can only operate on a balanced cash-flow basis, so the use of any tax revenue for cash payments to claimants, or equivalently by allowing use of certificates (bank books) for tax or public-utilities payments, even at deeply discounted rates, will only exacerbate a fiscal situation that is already under tremendous pressures. A proposed plan for resolving domestic claims is being discussed in the Federation (Box 3.1). Under the plan, domestic claims on the government would be limited by the stock of assets available for privatization. This plan has the advantage of minimizing the uncertainty of the large internal debt overhang; it also helps build political support for expanding private participation in the economy.

Box 3.1 Privatization and Resolution of Outstanding Claims

The most feasible method for resolving outstanding claims is to limit their use to the purchase of assets from privatization. In implementing this solution, it is crucial that the matching of claims to assets be performed as a one-time, coordinated decision that settles all outstanding claims against the government using the universe of all available assets. Other uses of privatization assets, such as compensating displaced homeowners, who might also have a claim on the state, must be included in this one-time settlement as well. Details on privatization strategies are described in Chapter VI.

Reforming the tax policies

Tax policy is characterized by extremely high and distortionary rates, particularly on wages and foreign trade, and numerous, arbitrary tax exemptions that have substantially narrowed the tax base. Payroll taxes on gross wages are between 45 and 50 percent, which is very high by international standards (Figure 3.1). Customs duties, including additional charges, are also excessive, particularly in Republika Srpska. These conditions demand a comprehensive reform of the tax system in the short term. Such a reform can be accomplished without any loss of revenues (Box 3.2).

Box 3.2 Revenue-neutral Tax Reform

The need for reform of the Bosnian tax system is apparent, with reducing taxation of labor and of imports as the major areas for reform. In addition, consideration should be given to adopting a value-added tax in place of the current sales taxes. Tax reform can be revenue neutral, meaning no revenues are lost as a consequence. It should be noted that a reform might be revenue neutral when it is first introduced, but the same reform is unlikely to be revenue neutral over time because of different growth rates in the before- and after-reform taxes. Revenue growth after reform must be adequate to provide for appropriate increases in public expenditures.

Taxation of labor through the wage tax and social contributions for health, pensions, unemployment, and other purposes results in a tax of about 50 percent on gross wages. The high tax rates discourage the use of labor, cause a tendency for nonreporting of employment and wages, and limit expansion of the private sector. The key to most tax reforms, including for wage taxes in Bosnia and Herzegovina, is reducing tax rates and broadening the bases to replace the revenue loss. The base for wage and income taxes can be broadened by including new items, such as fringe benefits, in the base and by achieving better compliance with tax laws

Taxation of imports is excessive in both Entities because of a combination of import duties that range up to more than 25 percent and excise tax rates, levied on alcohol, cigarettes, oil, and other products, that normally are much higher on imported than on domestic goods. International trade is discouraged and comparative advantages in Bosnia and Herzegovina are hidden by these attempts to protect domestic production. Import duties should be reduced to an average rate of 5 to 8 percent. Differential excise tax rates should be eliminated by raising domestic excise tax rates to the current levels imposed on imported products, and excise tax rates should be raised so that the new rate is as high as the combined old customs and excise tax rates. Higher excise tax rates on domestic production can help offset the revenue losses from lower import duties.

Bosnia and Herzegovina raises significant revenues through sales taxes. Development of a VAT in Bosnia and Herzegovina would require several years, but consideration should be given to such a reform. Most countries in the world have found a VAT to be preferred to sales taxes. Among other advantages, a VAT can have better compliance because of built in auditing characteristics and can help avoid the pyramiding of taxes that results from sales taxes that often are imposed on intermediate goods. Further, European Union members are not permitted to impose local sales taxes. A VAT would be most effectively collected by a tax administration at the State level.

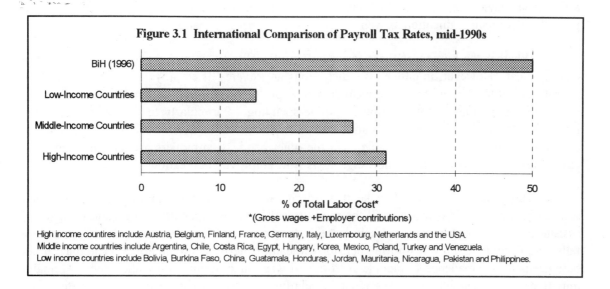

Figure 3.1 International Comparison of Payroll Tax Rates, mid-1990s

High income countires include Austria, Belgium, Finland, France, Germany, Italy, Luxemburg, Netherlands and the USA.
Middle income countries include Argentina, Chile, Costa Rica, Egypt, Hungary, Korea, Mexico, Poland, Turkey and Venezuela.
Low income countries include Bolivia, Burkina Faso, China, Guatamala, Honduras, Jordan, Mauritania, Nicaragua, Pakistan and Philippines.

High tax rates are undesirable for two reasons. First, they distort behavior. Employers either hire fewer workers because taxes raise the cost of labor, or they pay workers with nontaxable benefits such as food allowances and transportation. Similarly, the tax structure encourages capital formation at the expense of labor since enterprise tax rates are low (30 percent in Republika Srpska and 36 percent in the Federation) compared with the high tax rates on labor. High trade taxes inhibit exports, protect inefficient industries, and discourage the acquisition of foreign technology and capital. These distortions retard growth and exacerbate unemployment. Second, high taxes encourage tax evasion, further undermining the institutional structures that are essential for stable government.

Payroll taxes

Rate reductions are most critical for payroll taxes. Wage costs are about double the net wage in all parts of Bosnia and Herzegovina. Both Entities levy payroll taxes to fund pensions, health insurance, and unemployment compensation. Although that is standard practice in industrial countries, the rates are normally much lower. For example, the average combined payroll tax (as a percentage of gross wages plus employer contributions) in most industrial countries is about 30 percent, and much lower in some (see Figure 3.1).[5] Combined payroll tax rates for Bosnia and Herzegovina's three social funds alone are about 50 percent of gross wages.

In addition, both Entities levy other earmarked payroll taxes. Republika Srpska levies a general payroll tax (which could be transformed into an income tax) as well as a 2 percent payroll tax for social assistance and a 3 percent tax for infants' and children's benefits. In the Federation

---

[5]   The standard way to present payroll tax rates in the Organization for Economic Cooperation and Development (OECD) countries is as a percentage of pre-tax wages in which wages are measured gross of income taxes and other payroll tax deductions. Gross wages differ from total compensation, which includes all employer-paid taxes as well. In transition economies, wage-tax rates may be computed as a percentage of net wages or as a percentage of total compensation.

a 6 percent payroll tax is used to finance reconstruction; in the Bosnian Croat-majority areas payroll taxes finance education as well.

Whether the burden of these taxes falls principally on employers or on workers is not entirely clear. However, in either case, distortions are severe. If employers are able to pass the payroll tax on to workers by lowering their net wage, then essentially a small group of formal workers is supporting a large portion of public spending. Particularly to the extent that some informal or nonwage income opportunities are more lucrative than formal employment, such an outcome is regressive and inequitable. On the other hand, if employers are unable to pass the payroll tax on to workers, the higher wage costs slow employment creation.

The government should make it a priority to reduce payroll taxes and turn to other sources of revenue. This move is all the more urgent because expenditures on education, social assistance, and reconstruction are likely to be under pressure to rise faster than defense spending falls, and faster than reforms limiting pension or health benefits will take effect. The payroll tax base needs to be broadened to include all forms of wage income, including allowances. Equally important, wage and income taxes must be administered on private earnings. Together, the broader wage base, lower evasion and avoidance, and a rapidly expanding economy could replace much of the revenue lost to lower payroll tax rates.

Trade and excise taxes

Taxes on foreign trade are similarly excessive. Export taxes should be eliminated and import duties (ranging up to 32 percent in the Federation and even higher in Republika Srpska) should be reduced. Import duties should be no higher than 5-8 percent, and all items should be subject to a uniform tariff (see Chapter V). To compensate for the potential revenue loss revenue resulting from tariff reductions, excise tax rates should be raised so that the new rate is as high as the combined old customs and excise tax rates. In addition, excise tax rates should be imposed equally on imported goods and domestic production. These excise tax changes would easily offset much of the revenue losses from lower trade taxes.

Simplifying the tax structure would also facilitate compliance and administration. The Federation has made considerable progress in this area, reducing the number of sales taxes from 26 to 5. A new set of excise taxes has been imposed as well. Both Entities should move toward uniform sales taxes. A value-added tax or a tax on the sale to final consumers of all goods and services might be the best structure for a broad-based consumption tax. As discussed below, collection of any broad-based consumption tax, particularly a future value-added tax, would be facilitated if administration occurred at the State level.

Three Steps Are Required to Establish a Viable Institutional Framework for Fiscal Management

Sustainable fiscal policies need underpinned by sustainable institutional framework. A viable framework for fiscal management in Bosnia and Herzegovina will require securing financing for the State to cover administration and external debt service, coordinating inter-Equity fiscal policy and revenue collection, and assigning expenditure and revenue responsibilities with Entities.

Securing adequate and predictable financing for State administration and external debt service

Developing mechanisms to finance the State will be the first step towards sustainable fiscal policy. Although the Dayton Agreement outlined the division of fiscal responsibilities between the State and the Entities, many details need to be finalized (Box 3.3). Under the Agreement only foreign affairs, monetary policy, customs policy, debt management, and immigration are assigned to the State. Thus, in the near term the State budget will be small, since many traditional functions—such as defense and transfer payments—are assigned to the Entities. But since all significant taxing power resides with the two Entities, they must work together to provide adequate and predictable revenues to finance the State budget.[6]

Box 3.3 Fiscal Structure under the Dayton Agreement

Fiscal responsibilities agreed to under the Dayton Agreement are divided between the State and Entity governments and, in the case of the Federation, further divided among the Cantons. The most significant responsibility of the State government with respect to fiscal management is the payment of existing international financial obligations of Bosnia and Herzegovina, and of future international obligations incurred with the consent of both Entities. The State has no important independent revenue sources, and depends entirely on transfers from the two Entities--two thirds from the Federation and one third from Republika Srpska--to meet its obligations. There are, as yet, no permanent arrangements for these transfers, creating a serious problem for the country's debt management.

The Entity governments have exclusive responsibility in their territories over defense, internal affairs, economic and social-sector policies, resettlement and reconstruction, and justice, tax, and customs administration. Each Entity has ownership of the customs duties and excise taxes collected in its territory.

In the Federation, all responsibilities not assigned explicitly to the Entity government devolve to the cantons. These include education, culture, housing, public services, and social transfer expenditures. Each canton is authorized as well to delegate its responsibilities to the municipalities in its territory. Cantons are given ownership of sales, income, and property taxes, as well as of the fees charged for public services. Many cantons are far from being able to assume these responsibilities. Significant decisions have yet to be made regarding, first, the extent to which canton-level inequities in the provision of education and other services will be permitted; second, the extent to which joint provision or other arrangements will be pursued to ensure efficiency in the supply of public services; and third, the extent of intergovernmental transfers to support equity- and efficiency-enhancing arrangements.

Under a 1996 interim agreement between the Federation and the State, the State receives one third of the Federation's customs tax revenues. Starting in 1997, however, operational procedures should be implemented for setting the State budget and financing it through the Entities. The State's administrative budget is expected to be small in 1997. Under the Dayton Agreement, one third of the State budget will come from Republika Srpska and two thirds will come from the Federation; this arrangement should be implemented.

A separate budget or a separate part of the budget needs to be established to finance the State's debt service on restructured old debts (to international financial institutions and, soon, to the Paris and London Clubs) and on new borrowings by the State. The resources for servicing

---

[6] The State will receive some additional revenue from sources such as consular fees.

these debts and the mechanisms for securing and transferring funds to the state must be worked out to ensure smooth foreign financial relations. (Chapter IV discusses foreign-debt management in greater detail).

Looking beyond 1997, a mechanism will still be needed to provide the State with predictable and steady revenue. Longer-term options for funding the State budget include reassigning all or part of specific tax (such as customs duties) revenues or part of total tax revenues from the Entities to the State directly, periodically transferring funds from the Entity budgets to the State based on an agreed State budget, or a combination of these. Constitutional provisions might need to be revised for the State to collect revenues from specific taxes.

Coordinating fiscal policy and revenue collection between Entities

The Dayton Agreement calls for the dismantling of internal borders and customs posts between the two Entities, both to eliminate the costly economic inefficiencies of maintaining internal borders and to increase economic interactions and so contribute to political stability. Significant differences in customs and most other taxes would provide individuals and firms with incentives to avoid and evade taxes. Importation, production, and sales would shift to the lowest tax areas. The effects of differential tax rates would be mitigated if the Entities were prepared to cooperate to avoid destructive tax competition (competitive reductions in tax rates by each Entity to divert business from the other Entity) and to monitor evasive activities. In the foreign-trade area, the Dayton Agreement calls for State determination of uniform customs policies across Bosnia and Herzegovina--that is, no customs duties should be authorized that have not been approved by the State government. The next priority is for the Entity customs administrations to be linked and their work coordinated.

Other tax reforms, such as the possible introduction of a VAT in the future, should be shaped with similar concerns in mind. If production occurs in two Entities, VATs incurred in the Entity where the first stage of production takes place will be deducted from VATs incurred in the Entity where final production occurs. Administrative cooperation between the Entities will be needed to resolve conflicts over the magnitude and location of taxable production activity. When VAT rates are different, incentives for tax avoidance and the likelihood of inter-Entity disagreements about tax liabilities increase dramatically. Thus, rates for any future VAT should be set at the State level. Moreover, to minimize such inter-Entity administrative complexities, State administration of a future VAT is likely to prove advantageous.

Problems of unhealthy tax competition and administrative cooperation are less pronounced for excise taxes and import duties. For these taxes, the location of taxable activity (consumption) can be determined more easily, and the taxes are less subject to evasion. Commodities subject to excise taxes are usually handled by a small number of distributors, are produced by a few domestic firms, or are imported, so excise and import duties can be collected at one of these limited number of locations. Still, since many imports likely will enter through the borders of one Entity for consumption in the other, information must be collected at the border and from importers to ensure that import duties are directed to the appropriate Entity. Stamps and other identifiable markings can be placed on commodities to ensure that the tax on some commodities (such as cigarettes and alcohol) has been paid to the correct Entity. Pressures on administrative capacity will be eased considerably, however, if lower, uniform import duties were in place; incentives for abuse in the distribution of revenues across Entities would drop correspondingly. The assignment of taxes is discussed in greater detail in the following section.

Assigning responsibility for expenditures and revenues within the Entities

The Dayton Agreement provides for differences in the intra-Entity fiscal arrangements of the two Entities (Figure 3.2). The Federation's canton structure was intended to accommodate different demands for public services and to allow greater local control over service levels. Republika Srpska, in contrast, is expected to maintain its centralized approach. In both cases, allocating local public-expenditure responsibilities and revenue between the levels of government is a key policy issue. But, it is particularly relevant for the Federation, given its greater decentralization and the role cantons play in providing major social and governmental services.

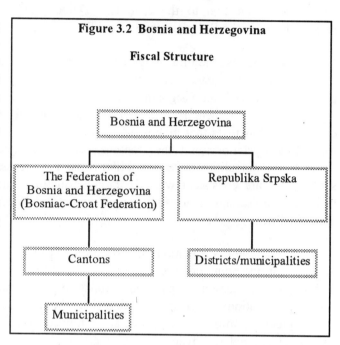

Figure 3.2 Bosnia and Herzegovina Fiscal Structure

Expenditures

Several considerations should govern the assignment of public-expenditure responsibilities between the State and Entities and between Entities and cantons and municipalities:

Efficiency: Public services that are most efficiently provided on a large scale (acute care hospitals, colleges, water treatment facilities) should be the responsibility of higher levels of government. Although in some cases local governments might be able to work together to provide these services efficiently, such cooperation is unlikely when there is political tension between jurisdictions.

Benefit spillovers: Public services that affect people who live outside the municipality or canton where the service is provided should be provided by higher levels of government. Sewage treatment facilities are sometimes in this category.

Differences in expenditure preferences: Preferences for local public expenditures might vary across jurisdictions. To the extent that they do, overall welfare is raised if lower levels of government have more control over public expenditures and can adjust them to the preferences of residents in different jurisdictions.

Equity: Local jurisdictions have different capacities to raise revenue. The greater are these differences, the larger are the inequities that result when jurisdictions must rely on local revenue sources to meet significant expenditure responsibilities. Having higher levels of government provide services or using intergovernmental grants to increase revenues in poorer areas can reduce interregional inequality. Dealing with these important equity considerations will be difficult given the low political tolerance for cross-subsidies.

The Dayton Agreement: The Dayton Agreement assigns responsibility for social welfare, health, and education to the cantons. Defense expenditures, on the other hand, are the responsibility of the Federation and Republika Srpska.

Making expenditure assignments therefore involves tradeoffs: equity and economic efficiency are often enhanced when higher levels of government are responsible for service provision, but such an assignment is not sustainable if local expenditure preferences diverge significantly or if there is little political tolerance for cross-subsidies. One assignment of expenditure functions that minimizes the cost of these tradeoffs is shown in Table 3.3. Since Republika Srpska does not have cantons, services assigned to the cantons need to be assigned either to municipalities or to Republika Srpska. The assignments listed in the table vary by service, but are consistent with the broad principles outlined above. For example, intercity highways are assigned to Entity governments, while secondary education is assigned to municipalities.

The 1994 Federation Constitution assigns several functions to the Federation government, including defense, federal police, justice, and customs administration. It would be reasonable to assign additional functions to the Entity governments, including telecommunications, university education, some health care, intercantonal transport, environmental control, and some social welfare functions (see Table 3.3). These services either have intercantonal spillovers or exhibit economies of scale that will not be exhausted at the cantonal level.

Table 3.3 Recommended Assignment of Public Functions

Service Category	Type of Service	Government Level
Heath care	Primary	Municipality
	Secondary (e.g., hospitals, curative)	Canton
	Tertiary (infectious disease, research)	Entity
Education	Primary	Municipality
	Secondary	Canton/Municipality
	University	Entity
Transportation	Roads/Highways (intracity)	Municipality
	Roads/Highways (intercity)	Canton
	Airports	Entity
	Public Transportation (intracity)	Municipality
	Public Transportation (intercity)	Entity
	Private Transportation, Taxis	Canton/Municipality
Environmental	Air/Water Pollution	Canton
	Water/Forestry	Entity/State
Housing	All	Canton
Solid waste, water, sewer, fire	All	Municipality/Canton
Land use/zoning	All	Municipality
Licensing/ regulation	All	Canton
Cultural policy	All	Canton
Tourism	All	Canton
Social welfare	All	Canton/Entity
Telecommunications	All	Entity/State

The Constitution makes cantons and municipalities responsible for services, including much of health care, education, housing, fire protection, and utilities. Since potential gains from large-scale production are limited and there are few interregional spillovers, assigning these functions to the Entities would not greatly increase economic efficiency. In addition, service preferences are likely to vary. But, the regions' different abilities to fund services will create significant inequities, exacerbating interjurisdictional tensions. Inequity could be eased by having Entities assume responsibilities for some locally assigned public expenditures and by providing intergovernmental grants to poor jurisdictions (cantons or municipalities). These approaches could create political difficulties, given that the political strains induced by the transfer system were a key contributor to the collapse of the former Yugoslavia. Thus, any transfer system designed to minimize large inequities must take great care to minimize potential sources of political tension. One fundamental requirement for easing tensions is to use objective and transparent indicators, to determine intergovernmental redistributions and to decide on Entity-level expenditures that affect jurisdictions differently.

Revenues and taxes

Several issues are involved in the implementation of a tax system: administering the tax, which includes collecting the tax, auditing taxpayers, and enforcing the tax law; defining the tax base and setting tax rates; and assigning ownership of revenue from the tax. In principle, policy making and revenue ownership for any tax administration can be assigned to different levels of government. The level of government that collects a tax does not have to be the one that sets the tax rate or gets the revenue. For example, revenue from State or federally imposed and collected taxes can be—and, in other countries often is—shared with lower levels of government.

As with expenditure responsibilities, several criteria affect the assignment of tax revenues:

- Each level of government must be able to fund the services for which it is responsible. Some cantons (municipalities) will not be able to meet their expenditure obligations for the taxes over which they are assigned ownership under the Dayton Agreement. As a result some transfers from the Entity (canton) will need to be considered, either in the form of budget transfers or the assignment of revenues from taxes collected by higher-level governments.

- For some important taxes it is difficult to define the canton or municipality where the taxable activity occurs. For example, for the corporate income tax, the taxable activity could be defined as taking place where the corporate headquarters is located, where the work force or capital is concentrated, or where sales are concentrated. This ambiguity will make it difficult to divide the revenue between different cantons or municipalities; thus, the revenue should be assigned to higher levels of government.

- Governments have few incentives to set rates efficiently and invest resources in tax collection if tax revenues flow elsewhere. For example, cantons will exert less effort to collect sales taxes if they do not receive revenue from them.

- Near-term decisions on revenue assignments are fixed in the Dayton Agreement and the Constitution; these arrangements create considerations in addition to the economic criteria listed above.

Administrative capacity is a significant constraint on many countries, including Bosnia and Herzegovina. Given scarce administrative capacity, the most efficient way to administer and collect many major taxes (customs, excise, wage, personal income) is to centralize collection at least at the Entity level and, in the case of customs taxes, eventually at the State level. Thus, the current practice of using municipal tax collection offices in the Bosnian, Croat, and Serb areas needs to be reconsidered over the medium term. About 90 tax offices operate in the Federation and 60 in Republika Srpska. One argument for this system is that local offices have better information for determining tax liabilities. But using such a large number of offices is an inefficient way to collect taxes in a modern economy, a handicap that should be reorganized as tax administrations are reformed and modernized.

Further, for the most important taxes (including excise, corporate income, personal income, and sales taxes), the tax base should be defined and tax rates should be set at the Entity level with the two Entities working together to define these variables as similarly as possible. Entity-level determinations of tax rates and bases are preferable for these important taxes for these reasons:

- Uniform rates and bases make tax administration easier for the government and tax compliance easier for corporations and individuals involved in cross-jurisdictional business.

- Tax competition might cause costly rate-cutting wars if lower levels of government set tax rates or define the tax base, if the taxable activity or factor of production is mobile. Should this occur, there will be efficiency losses due to tax avoidance and a significant erosion of the fiscal base.[7]

- However, when the potential for tax competition is small and when tax administration can be handled more efficiently at the local level (such as with property taxes and real estate transfers), allowing local governments latitude over bases and rates will allow different jurisdictions to satisfy different preferences for local public services.

Table 3.4 summarizes a set of tax assignments that is consistent with these criteria. The rules for revenue ownership mandated in the Dayton Agreement are reflected in the final column. However, tax assignments should not be expected to remain in place indefinitely, given that demands for services, and revenues from taxes, change over time. Still, any assignment should be maintained for a reasonable period of time to ensure predictable revenue flows.

Two examples illustrate the logic behind the tax and revenue assignments. First, Entities should set the basic rates for wage and personal income taxes, and cantons should be allowed to impose surcharges. This approach gives cantons some flexibility while reducing the potential for rates being driven downward by tax competition. Since it is easy to measure where the taxable activity occurs (for example, where the worker works, for payroll tax purposes), revenues could easily be assigned to cantons or municipalities, as well as to the Entities.

Second, municipal governments should set tax rates and be assigned revenues for real estate and property taxes. Since the tax base is immovable, municipalities could set their own rates, within reasonable bounds, without risking excessive tax competition. And, since the location of real estate is clearly defined, assigning the revenue to the municipalities is consistent

---

[7]   Although many countries have decentralized tax systems, the political reality in Bosnia and Herzegovina makes ad hoc interjurisdictional cooperation more difficult than in many other countries.

with the above criteria. Municipal governments also might administer the tax, since they will probably find tasks such as valuing property easier and less expensive than would higher levels of government.

Table 3.4 Summary of Suggested Tax Assignments

Tax Type	Tax Administration	Tax Base and Tax Rates	Revenue Ownership
Customs	Entity	State	Entity*
Excises	Entity	Entity; surcharges by canton or municipality	Entity, canton or municipality at retail level
Wage and personal income	Entity or canton	Entity; surcharges by canton	Entity, canton, and municipality*
Corporate income	Entity	Entity	Entity
Sales tax (retail level)	Entity; feasible but difficult for cantons	Entity; surcharges by canton	Entity, canton and municipality*
Property tax	Municipality	Municipality	Municipality*
Real estate transfers	Municipality	Municipality	Municipality*
Motor vehicles	Municipality	Canton	Canton and municipality
Social Security contributions	Entity	Entity	Funds
User Fees, Social Services	Service provider	Canton or municipality	Service provider
User Fees, Utilities	Service supplier	Service supplier (subject to regulation)	Service supplier
VAT	State	State	State, Entity, canton

* The Constitution assigns revenues from Excise and Customs to the Entities and sales, income, and property taxes in the Federation to the Cantons. Therefore, these recommendations require the appropriate governments to reach revenue sharing agreements.

Implementing tax and revenue assignments consistent with these recommendations and the Dayton Agreement will require considerable progress in cantonal and municipal organization. Although all 10 of the Federation's cantons have been legally established in at least a rudimentary form, some (notably Tuzla, Bihać, and Zenica) are more advanced. Large administrations have been formed in these cantons, with Tuzla having more than 250 employees and Bihać about 140. Other cantons have elected a parliament and a president and have appointed the cantonal cabinet. However, they still have to determine their responsibilities relative to their constituent municipalities. In Republika Srpska, municipalities share in tax revenue under sharing formulas established by Republika Srpska's Parliament. The payments bureau transfers revenues directly to municipal accounts according to those formulas. Although these developments are important, much more needs to be done to develop transparent rules for intergovernmental transfers and to appropriately assign government expenditure responsibilities.

Chapter IV

External Debt Management

To a large extent, Bosnia and Herzegovina's access to external financing will depend on early resolution of its debt problems and the effectiveness of external borrowing arrangements. Creditors avoid countries where legal and institutional arrangements are uncertain, procedures for decision making in borrowing are unclear, and monitoring of debt transactions is weak. Only with a strong debt-management system will Bosnia and Herzegovina be able to diversify its sources of external finance to contain the cost of borrowing once grant financing is depleted. Such a system will require clarifying responsibilities for foreign borrowing between the State and its two Entities and ensuring debt service through efficient legal and institutional arrangements.

Dayton Agreement Laid Out a Broad Framework for External Borrowing

The Constitution adopted as part of the Dayton Agreement provides certain parts of the comprehensive framework that is required for external borrowing (Box 4.1). Borrowing authority and debt servicing are covered only generally, however. Two clauses are particularly important in determining the constitutional framework for external borrowing: one recognizes the State government as responsible for international obligations; and the other recognizes the Entities as responsible for providing the State government with the financial assistance it needs to honor these obligations.

Box 4.1 Bosnia and Herzegovina: Constitutional Provisions on External Borrowing

The Constitution incorporates the following clauses on external borrowing:

Article III lists as one of the responsibilities of the Government of Bosnia and Herzegovina: "Finances of the institutions and for the international obligations of Bosnia and Herzegovina. . ."

Article III lists as one of the responsibilities of the Entities: to "provide all necessary assistance to the government of Bosnia and Herzegovina in order to enable it to honor the international obligations of Bosnia and Herzegovina..."

Article IV assigns to the Parliamentary Assembly responsibility for "deciding upon the sources and amounts of revenues for the operations of the institutions of Bosnia and Herzegovina and international obligations of Bosnia and Herzegovina."

Article VIII states that the "Parliamentary Assembly shall each year, on the proposal of the Presidency, adopt a budget covering the expenditures required to carry out the responsibilities of the institutions of Bosnia and Herzegovina and the international obligations of Bosnia and Herzegovina."

Article VIII specifies that the "Federation shall provide two thirds, and the Republika Srpska one third, of the revenues required by the budget, except insofar as revenues are raised as specified by the Parliamentary Assembly."

Finally, the Constitution states that "each Entity may also enter into agreements with states and international organizations with the consent of the Parliamentary Assembly."

Another important provision in the Dayton Agreement relating to debt management is that the State has no independent tax authority unless Parliament grants it. This and other provisions impose serious constraints on the design of the debt-management system (see Box 4.1). For example, separate borrowing and debt-servicing authorities create a specific free-rider problem: if one Entity defaults, both the State and the other Entity's ability to borrow will be jeopardized. To address the free-rider problem, the link between the borrowing authority and debt-servicing mechanism must be exceptionally strong. The efficiency of external debt-servicing arrangements will crucially depend on the parties' commitment to cooperation.

Two issues must be clarified in order to establish an effective external borrowing arrangement within the broad framework provided in the Constitution: the borrowing authority and modalities; and the debt-servicing mechanism.

External borrowing responsibilities

Borrowing arrangements must take into account both the preferences of creditors and the fiscal arrangements in Bosnia and Herzegovina. Many creditors, particularly those holding old claims, might prefer or be obliged to conduct their financial relations through State-level institutions. For example, for multilateral institutions like the World Bank and the International Monetary Fund, the sovereign borrowing authority is the State which is constitutionally recognized as responsible for international obligations and is a statutory member of both institutions. But, under the highly decentralized structure created by the Dayton Agreement, the Entities are able to tax and collect customs duties and so have greater fiscal capacity and greater ability to service debt. Precluding the Entities from external borrowing that is not guaranteed by the State would create an extremely centralized borrowing modality in which each Entity potentially has veto power over borrowing by the other Entity. Such an arrangement is unrealistic under current circumstances.

Thus, a law on external debt needs to be adopted to clarify the mandates and functions at each level of government and identify subsidiary responsibilities of Entities and Entity institutions. Such a law is being prepared by the Debt Negotiation Committee, which includes representatives from the State and the two Entities. The draft law details the responsibilities of the State and the Entities in external debt management and the coordination mechanisms between them. This legislative work has benefited from significant support from the Office of Technical Assistance of the U.S. Treasury.

Under the arrangement being considered, the State will be able to borrow on its own with Parliamentary approval. The State will also be able to borrow on behalf of the Entities. The Entities will be able to borrow by themselves as well (without State guarantee). Direct external borrowing by the Entities has the status of local government borrowing. Since the State has a narrow fiscal base and will not be able to support borrowing on its own, the legislation provides for the cross-indemnification of State borrowings by the Entities.

Once economic recovery is well advanced, a significant portion of investment needs may be financed by private external lending to private economic agents. Lending to public institutions such as cantons or public enterprises could also be allowed, without necessarily involving the State or Entities. Such lending can be guaranteed with State parliamentary approval. Over the next few years, the nongovernment sector might be able to borrow externally only with a payment guarantee from the government.

The proposed debt-servicing mechanism will enhance Bosnia and Herzegovina's credit-worthiness

Establishing a clear budget mechanism for debt service, both for new borrowing and restructured old debt, is also crucial to implementing the proposed legislative framework and ensuring the maintenance of normal relations with foreign creditors. Given the State's weak fiscal base, its credence as a sovereign borrowing authority would be impaired without a robust debt-servicing mechanism.

Under the debt-management setup established by the draft legislation, the State would service external debt with resources provided by the Entities. The Entities will collect customs duties and taxes, and, therefore, will retain ultimate control over debt-servicing capacity. The Entities will transfer resources to the State budget to service three categories of debt: loans contracted directly by the State; loans contracted by the State on behalf of the Entities; and restructured old debts. The legislation being prepared incorporates several mechanisms to address the free-rider problem, the establishment of a mechanism to facilitate stable cash flows from Entities to the State, and servicing of restructured old debt.

Free-rider problem. The draft law qualifies only the State's external borrowing as sovereign debt. Thus, state debt has seniority over any other external borrowing by the Entity, cantonal, and other local governments. Under the Constitution, the Entities are obligated to provide resources to service the State's external debt, both that inherited from the former Yugoslavia and that contracted by Bosnia and Herzegovina itself. The State's borrowing is controlled by the Parliamentary Assembly, with representation from all parts of the country.

Transfer of resources from Entities to the State for debt service. External debt service is treated by the legislation as a permanent and indefinite appropriation from each Entity's budget. Entities must provide to the State estimates of their revenues prior to the start of each fiscal year, and the State will supply to them estimates of future debt-service needs. During the year the resources required for debt-service payments will be transferred by the Entities to a special debt-servicing account managed by the Central Bank (probably by the way of the Payment Bureau). These transfers might be derived from any given stream of tax revenues, or might come in the form of payments by the end-user enterprise to which the State and the institution had passed the borrowed funds. The responsibility for debt-service payments to external creditors rests with the governments that contracted the debt, not with the enterprises that used the funds. To ensure transparency of debt-service flows, transfers to the State from the Entities for debt service will likely be separate from those for the State administrative budget.

Dealing with old debt. Transparent debt-servicing mechanisms are essential for successful renegotiation of old debt, a pressing task confronting the State government. In the process of defining the debt-management arrangements, both Entities have agreed to divide the debt-service payments according to the final beneficiary principle. The Entities have not, however, worked out a debt-service ratio on the basis of this principle. The draft legislation requires that the Entities work out the division of debt-service responsibilities by May 1997. This arrangement enhances the credibility of the debt-servicing mechanism and, therefore, facilitates the renegotiation of the external debt of Bosnia and Herzegovina.

Setting Up a New Debt-Management System at the State Level Is Critical

Establishing a debt-management unit at the State level is a priority. The unit must focus on two urgent tasks: rescheduling the stock of old debt; and managing the new financing that will increasingly flow in on loan terms rather than as grants. The unit should have three main functions:

- Preparing and negotiating loan agreements and monitoring the use and repayment of government and government-guaranteed loans;

- Developing and implementing an external debt recording system and monitoring all government and government-guaranteed loans, including the keeping of a debt ledger and producing of debt reports; and

- Formulating proposals for debt strategy and policy, including setting an annual borrowing limit and determining sustainable borrowing levels. This function includes the analysis of major borrowing policy issues, the monitoring of developments in international finance, and debt renegotiation.

The debt management unit will maintain a database of all State debt obligations, monitor compliance with terms and conditions of external debt arrangements, prepare assessments for the Entity governments on their shares of debt service, and monitor deposits to the State debt-servicing account by the tax-levying governments. Should the required transfers to the debt-servicing account fall short of what is needed, the unit will notify the relevant agencies and take other actions to protect the regularity of debt-service payments. As the portfolio of external obligations grows, other functions, such as risk management, may be added.

In the longer term, the unit will have to elaborate proposals for the national borrowing strategy, which will be adopted and implemented by the State government in close consultation with the Entities. A key element of the borrowing strategy is the annual borrowing limit, adopted as part of the annual budget. The borrowing limit should be based on estimates of the country's long-term capacity to incur and carry debt. The limit should include all forms of borrowing, including loans taken directly and those guaranteed by the State. These estimates will be a key task for the debt-management unit.

Since part of the State's external borrowing may be undertaken on behalf of the Entities, and since the Entities will borrow on their own, Entity Ministries of Finance will need to monitor their own obligations as well as the obligations of enterprises located on their territory. To do so, the ministries will need to establish their own debt-monitoring units. The State's debt-management unit and the Entities' debt-monitoring units will have to cooperate closely, preparing assessments of the future debt service.

At the policymaking level, it might be useful to establish a high-level coordination committee to reconcile the varying interests of groups and industries as end users of borrowed resources. This committee should have senior representation from all relevant agencies, at both the State and Entity levels. The Debt Negotiation Committee is a good prototype for such a high-level coordination body.

Chapter V

Foreign Trade and Customs Administration

Foreign-trade policy is an important component of economic management in all countries. Its relative importance to Bosnia and Herzegovina is particularly great given the country's small size and special circumstances. In small countries imports and exports tend to account for large portions of GDP. Since Bosnia and Herzegovina's industrial base has been completely disrupted by the breakup of the former Yugoslavia and severely damaged by the war, trade policy will be very important in determining the sectoral composition of economic growth as well as the rate of growth itself. Rapid development of exports is particularly important to generate both employment and the foreign exchange required to finance imports.

Creating a Liberal and Transparent Trade Regime Is a High Priority

A high level of trade dependency and export-led growth would not be new for the economy. Before the war, the economy was closely integrated with the former Yugoslav economy and, to a lesser extent, with the socialist bloc and the rest of the world. A wide variety of Bosnian products were exported, some directly and some through former Yugoslav trading companies located outside Bosnia and Herzegovina. Trade with Eastern Europe and the former Soviet Union was extensive, albeit usually on the basis of bilateral trade arrangements rather than driven by market forces.

This trading experience of many firms in both Entities should prove an important asset in rapidly rebuilding export markets. But, prewar trade was often based on political decisions about the location of industrial investments or on extensive direct and indirect forms of subsidization and protection. In part because the conduct of world trade has changed substantially in the 1990s, and in part because of tighter budgetary resources than in the past, both the conduct and patterns of Bosnian foreign trade will need to adjust.

In 1996, both the Federation and Republika Srpska showed signs that trade is growing rapidly, albeit from very low levels, especially in the Federation. Most of the increase, however, is in imports of consumption goods and fuels. Imports of industrial raw materials and intermediate goods and export growth are lagging, corresponding to low capacity utilization. In 1996, total merchandise exports were estimated at US$336 million and imports at US$1,882 million. This massive trade deficit is being financed by direct foreign aid, by the local spending of foreigners (including UN and Special Forces (SFOR) personnel), and by remittances. Over time, these sources will diminish, and imports will need to be financed increasingly by export earnings.

Thus, the authorities must quickly introduce and maintain a sound foreign-trade regime that allows enterprises operating in free markets to determine what will be traded and with whom. Such a regime is essential for rapidly restoring export growth and maximizing the potential gains from trade opportunities. The following sections review the current policies and arrangements for regulating foreign trade and identify needed reforms.

The Two Entities Have Adopted Different Policies and Procedures

Republika Srpska's foreign-trade law is patterned on the laws of the Federal Republic of Yugoslavia; the Federation's law is patterned on the laws of the Republic of Croatia. Both Croatia's and Yugoslavia's laws are in turn modified versions of the laws of the former Socialist Federal Republic of Yugoslavia. These laws give the governments considerable discretion in managing and directing trade. Both Entities have laws covering licensing requirements and classifying import and export goods into three categories: those that can be bought or sold without restriction, those requiring licenses, and those subject to quotas on physical quantities or values. In addition, there are a variety of trade taxes, duties, and excise taxes. Governments have wide authority to grant exemptions, which are widespread. There are also foreign-exchange restrictions on the Bosnian dinar (used in Bosnia-majority areas) and the Yugoslav dinar (widely used in Republika Srpska).

Although the legal framework for foreign trade is broadly similar in the two Entities, the Federation has gone further in liberalizing its regime (Table 5.1). Federation authorities report that exports are not subject to any quotas, taxes, or tariffs, or special licensing requirements. In addition, there are no quotas on imports. There are, however, licensing requirements for imports of pharmaceuticals, weapons, and certain categories of livestock and agricultural goods (mainly for reproductive purposes). The Federation had adopted Croatia's tariff rate structure, with an average tariff of about 13 percent.[8] In addition, there are stamp taxes, a general 10 percent levy to finance reconstruction, and special excise regimes on goods such as fuels. The government can grant exemptions for general categories or case by case. For example, firms engaging in reconstruction activities do not have to pay the 10 percent reconstruction tax. Since it is impossible to conclusively define reconstruction activities, this exemption opens the door to abuse.

Table 5.1 Simple Average Tariff Rate in the Entities of BiH, end 1996

	Simple Average		Simple Average Applied Rate		Standard Deviation	
	Federation	RS	Federation	RS	Federation	RS
Agricultural products, fish	2.7	8.7	12.7	26.7	2.6	5.1
Industrial products	3.0	11.1	13.0	29.1	2.9	5.3
Total	3.0	10.5	13.0	28.5	2.8	5.3

Source: Derived from data compiled by the European Union Customs and Fiscal Assistance Office in Sarajevo.
Note : Agricultural products cover chapters 1 through 25 of the Combined Nomenclature.

Republika Srpska maintains import quotas on certain foods, tobacco and alcohol products, and fuels. The authorities consider these items important primarily because of their role in promoting the recovery of domestic industries and anticipate their removal once recovery has occurred. In addition, Republika Srpska has adopted the tariffs used by the Federal Republic of Yugoslavia, which are much higher on average (28.5 percent on an unweighted basis) than those in the Federation and vary widely for protectionist reasons.[9] Exemptions are apparently

---

[8]   Imports from Croatia are duty-free and subject only to a 1 percent tax.

[9]   Imports from the FRY are duty-free and subject only to a 1 percent tax.

widespread, however. There are also export quotas and taxes on certain raw materials such as livestock, meat, dairy produce, products of the milling industry, tobacco products, ores, slag and ash, works of art, and antiques. However, there are few quantitative restrictions for industrial manufactures. They affect selected leather products and wood products.

During the war, Bosnia and Herzegovina's customs administration was split into three administrations: the Republika Srpska administration, the Bosniac administration in the Bosniac-majority areas, and the Croat administration in the Croat-majority areas. In 1996, a unified Federation Customs Administration was established, replacing the Bosniac and Croat administrations. There was also some limited coordination between the Republika Srpska administration and the Federation administration. Nevertheless, with different administrative procedures and infrastructure facilities between the two administrations, there is an increasing danger of mismanagement of customs revenue collection and tax evasions.

Trade Policies Must Be Reintegrated and Reformed

Cross-country evidence demonstrates that trade protection measures are costly and rarely effective. The benefits of liberalizing foreign trade are perhaps clearest in the transition economies moving from socialism to market economies. Radical trade liberalization has occurred throughout Central and Eastern Europe and in countries of the former Soviet Union. Tariff levels have been reduced, and quotas, licenses, and special lists have been scrapped almost entirely. These adjustments have been accompanied by rapid growth in trade (especially of exports to the West), which has been the leading component of economic growth in almost every transition economy. Cross-country studies also indicate that trade reform is most sustainable— that is, least likely to be reversed—when deep reforms and liberalization are introduced rapidly rather than gradually.

Bosnia and Herzegovina should initiate trade reforms as soon as possible. The main liberalization steps--reducing tariffs and removing nontariff trade barriers--should occur now, ahead of the recovery rather than being introduced gradually, as industrial output recovers. Otherwise, trade policy that leads to distorted relative prices among tradable goods will also distort the allocation of resources. And, once enterprises get used to protection, it is exceedingly difficult to remove it.

The Federation and Republika Srpska rely on customs duties for 10 to 15 percent of their budget revenues. Since lowering trade taxes should be an essential feature of a comprehensive liberalization program, this large share presents a dilemma. At a minimum, all exemptions should be eliminated to allow average rates to fall. In addition, as discussed in the fiscal policy section, there are feasible ways of replacing most (if not all) customs revenues with broad-based, less distortionary taxes, some of which (such as excise taxes) could be administered using the customs services. This arrangement illustrates the link between different aspects of policy that require reform. The Dayton Agreement requires the State to determine a uniform customs policy and a common external tariff with the rest of the world. Until now, foreign-exchange restrictions have been an important trade barrier except in the Croat-controlled portions of the Federation that use the Croatian kuna. These restrictions can be eliminated once the new Central Bank is established as a currency board, since the currency board system requires full convertibility on the current account.

At the State level, the agenda in foreign trade should be to:

- Establish a common external tariff structure that has nearly uniform rates and as low an average rate as possible (say 8 percent for all goods), with no exemptions;

- Enact a new foreign-trade law that would limit (in both Entities) the scope for intervention and limit quantitative restrictions to cases where health or safety issues are involved; and

- Negotiate accession to the World Trade Organization and broker agreements on trade liberalization with other trading partners (such as the European Union).

The first step is the preparation and adoption of relevant laws governing foreign trade. The laws being prepared now include the Law on Foreign Trade Policy, the Law on Customs Policies, and the Law on Customs Tariffs. The State and Entity governments should not be directly involved in conducting trade or in negotiating commercial agreements on behalf of local governments or Bosnian firms. Moreover, the Entity governments should refrain from extending exemptions from the remaining trade taxes.

The Entities need not wait until the common trade policy law being prepared is adopted by the State parliament to accelerate their liberalization programs. Measures can be taken immediately to reduce the governments' discretion in imposing trade restrictions. Tariffs can be lowered at the same time that other indirect taxes are broadened in base or raised in rates. Procedures for registering, licensing, and handling foreign exchange can be simplified. In Republika Srpska, all quotas and taxes on exports should be eliminated. In the Federation, licensing procedures should meet European standards.

Under the Dayton Agreement, customs administration is to be conducted at the Entity level. Tax evasion can be limited and revenues remitted to the appropriate government if the Entities cooperate. To this end, the administrative procedures of the two Entities should be harmonized to the greatest extent possible, and parallel investments should be made to upgrade the infrastructure facilities for both administrations on a simultaneous basis.

Part Two

Moving Toward A Market Economy

Reconstruction and economic recovery in Bosnia and Herzegovina are too big a task for the public sector alone. A key element of economic reform is to continue the transition to a market economy with a vibrant private sector. Regional experience has shown that such a transition requires simultaneous effort in three related areas: privatizing State- and socially-owned assets, developing a supportive business environment for private firms, and creating a disciplined and competitive financial sector. The Entity governments will play the leading role in these efforts, though some coordination mechanisms for inter-Entity issues at the State level will also be needed. Both Entities have moved forward rapidly in developing the legal framework for mass privatization of enterprises. Now, they must develop the institutional capacity to implement the programs. Coherent laws, functioning courts, and predictable tax administration are also needed to encourage foreign investment and domestic entrepreneurship. These changes imply a new paradigm for the government's role in the economy—rather than controlling the economy, the government must now manage it. As the government sheds its role of inefficient producer, it can focus on providing social services and other public goods and regulating productive activities.

Large conglomerates dominated Bosnia and Herzegovina's prewar economy. Most parts of many conglomerates are no longer viable due to physical damage, obsolete technology, and lost markets. Major structural changes in the economies of trading partners mean that the demand for some conglomerates' output has diminished. Price distortions that prevailed prior to the war are no longer there or are being removed. And, subsidies and trade protection that were essential to the viability of some activities have been phased out or should be in the near future. The challenge will be for each Entity to identify the parts of the conglomerate that are salvageable—that is, activities for which markets exist and private investors can be found— and to move them as quickly as possible into the private sector. Doing so will require changing laws, clarifying investment regulations, and adopting a flexible posture and realistic expectations on what the newly-privatized companies will produce and how much employment they will generate.

The financial sector poses additional challenges. There are 53 small banks operating in Bosnia and Herzegovina; 42 are in the Federation and 11 in Republika Srpska. Most of these banks are insolvent, with uncollectable loans far outstripping capital. Structural problems and war damage have led to a crisis in the banking sector that must be addressed. Moreover, many of these banks have limited experience with managing credit and mobilizing deposits and currently focus on generating-fee income from transfers and other services. Progress on bank monitoring and supervision must be continued. Rapid privatization or liquidation of the socially-owned banks must take place. In addition, the infusion of significant amounts of capital and know-how, the entry of well-capitalized new banks, and the creation of a stronger framework for financial regulation and bankruptcy and collateral laws will be crucial elements of banking-sector reform.

Chapter VI

Privatization and Private-Sector Development

Before the war, Bosnia and Herzegovina and the rest of the former Yugoslavia were a major gateway between the former Soviet bloc and Western economies. Bosnia and Herzegovina had a well-developed industrial economy, ranking among the leaders of the region. During the nearly four years of war, however, much of the industrial infrastructure was damaged or destroyed. In addition, the global shift away from state planning and protection is forcing enterprises to adjust their management, organization, and orientation to new economic realities. Prewar Bosnia and Herzegovina contained about 1,000 industrial organizations employing nearly 450,000 people—accounting for about half of total employment outside agriculture (Table 6.1). Heavy and light industries accounted for 43 percent of GDP in 1990, higher than in any other former Yugoslav republics. Industrial activities were concentrated in Sarajevo, Mostar, Zenica, and Tuzla. The most important industries were in iron ore production and processing, coal, ferrous and nonferrous metal production, machinery, forestry, and wood processing. Heavy industry was already in decline before 1992 with the fading of the cold war. Light industries included food processing, construction, and the manufacture of textile products, leather goods, and shoes. Overall, industrial activities were concentrated in a small number of firms: a dozen large industrial conglomerates accounted for up to 35 percent of GDP prior to the war.

The largest enterprises also dominated exports. In 1989, for example some 40 percent of the former Yugoslavia's export earnings were generated by four industrial conglomerates in present-day Bosnia and Herzegovina. In contrast with many Central and Eastern European economies, many of the prewar conglomerates had joint venture agreements with international companies, including Volkswagen, Daimler-Benz, and Olivetti.

These arrangements did not guarantee high productivity, however. By some accounts, prewar productivity in the best firms was 60 percent of that in Western European competitors, and the norm for public enterprises was only about 40 percent of productivity relative to Western competitors. These companies relied on cheap labor and large-scale subsidies to compensate for their inefficiency. Despite its heavy industrialization, Bosnia and Herzegovina was the second- poorest region of the former Yugoslavia, after Macedonia.

Table 6.1 Bosnia and Herzegovina: Industrial Structure, 1990

Sector	Employment	Output (tons)
Textiles	76,000	
Cotton fabric		13,000
Knitted fabric		7,000
Garments		2,800,000 sq. m.
Leather Products	28,000	
Shoes		710,000 pairs
Chemicals	19,000	
Ammonium Nitrate		84,000
Ammonium Sulfate		13,000
Soap and Detergent		52,000
Machine Building	80,000	
Iron Castings		63,000
Metals		
Aluminum	5,100	89,000
Steel (Raw)	26,000	1,500,000

Note: The 1990 structure of Bosnian industry included the above major sectors according to UNIDO (1996).

Before the war Bosnia and Herzegovina (and the former Yugoslavia) had taken steps toward a more market-oriented economy, granting greater autonomy to socially- and State-owned enterprises, encouraging explicit employee ownership of enterprise shares, and liberalizing conditions for setting up and operating private enterprises. Enterprise managers enjoyed considerable autonomy because most capital was designated as "social"—formally under the control of workers, but effectively under the control of managers.[10] Under this system, some managers were able to increase their enterprise's global market share, develop new products and technologies, and pursue profit-ability. But, the lack of accountability meant that many managers could perform poorly for extended periods or pursue noncommercial goals without having to bear negative consequences. Large enterprises were shareholders or owners of banks and had easy access to loans from these banks. Furthermore, it was considered part of the social responsibility of enterprises to create and maintain employment; efficiency was hardly acknowledged as a primary goal. Thus, even with the implementation of reforms during the prewar period, firms were only slightly exposed to market-based incentives.

The War Had Far Reaching Effects on Industry

The war affected firms in a number of ways. Many factories were damaged. Some of this damage has been repaired, but much of it cannot be, because of landmines around plants and equipment, loss of critical personnel, or changes in market conditions. Infrastructure was also damaged throughout the country, and much of it remains in disrepair. Skilled workers are in short supply. Nine of ten industrial workers were either in the armed forces or were physically displaced during the war. Many former workers—including some of the most skilled and best educated—are refugees abroad and are unlikely to return in the near future.

Because of these problems, manufacturing output after the war was initially at only about 5 percent of prewar levels. Factories that are operating report capacity utilization averaging around 40 percent, but that is based on the capacity that remains in the wake of the war's destruction. There have also been many permanent closures. As a result, exports from Bosnia and Herzegovina have declined dramatically. In a recent World Bank survey, a broad cross-section of Federation firms reported exporting an average of only 3 percent of their total output, and industrial firms roughly 5 percent.[11] Republika Srpska firms, which were not cut off from traditional trade links through Federal Republic of Yugoslavia (Serbia-Montenegro) during the war, report exporting 53 percent of their (substantially reduced) output.[12]

---

[10] The 1988-89 Marković program, distributed enterprise shares to both workers and managers. In principle, workers councils managed the firms, but in practice managers appear to have maintained control.

[11] This survey was part of the World Bank's Private Sector Assessment "New Foundations: Private Sector Development in Post-War Bosnia and Herzegovina, February 1997" which was undertaken to evaluate the role of the private sector in the economy and to identify constraints to its competitive operation and growth.

[12] The Republika Srpska sample was disproportionately concentrated among industrial firms, and hence may overstate the role of exports in the overall economy. However, international trade is likely to play an important role in any small nation lacking certain basic industries.

Other changes have affected the way firms are managed. During the war, enterprises lost much of their prewar autonomy. State ownership was reasserted over most enterprises, and the authorities reverted to appointing directors and managers. Thus, public enterprises emerged from the war not only physically devastated by destruction, theft, and sabotage, but also constrained by government control.

Because socially- and State-owned enterprises were major customers of private enterprises, they are also suffering from the devastation of the sector. Equally important, events during and after the war have made private enterprises almost entirely domestically oriented. The war's destruction of infrastructure and interruption of trade links, followed by the recently heightened domestic demand created by aid and remittance inflows, has left most businesses with little ability or incentive to enter global markets. Many firms report that they are unable to reestablish links with former trade partners because they are regarded as unreliable or uncompetitive. In this environment, firms are losing opportunities for renewed trade as well as the production technology and managerial know-how that comes with international partnerships and trade.

Privatizing Enterprises and Redefining the Government's Role

Privatization is at the top of the reform agenda in both Entities.[13] All parties recognize that the private sector must play a critical role in revitalizing the economy. Thus, Bosnia and Herzegovina needs to act systematically to improve its environment for private business—transforming the government into an efficient supporter of private production, creating the financial, legal, and institutional underpinnings for private investment and exchange, and actively working to restore trade and investment links to the rest of the world. This new role does not mean that the government will become less important. It does mean, however, that in many respects the government must "get out of the way" of private firms, and increase its support for the development of competitive markets. Much of the anticipated increase in private activity will come from the privatization of activities now being carried out by socially- or State-owned enterprises. But, even more will come about as a result of new private entry into many areas of the economy. Thus, it is essential that supportive proper legal and regulatory frameworks be put in place.

Preparation for privatization in the Federation is proceeding well

According to recent data from the Statistical Office, 2,288 enterprises in the Federation are candidates for privatization (Table 6.2). Most are large or strategic enterprises (based on either the number of employees or registered capital stock).

Circumstances have permitted close scrutiny over the past 10-12 months of Federation plans for privatization, during which time considerable progress has been made. Critical legislation affecting privatization includes the Privatization Agency Law, the Law on the Privatization of Enterprises, the Law on Restitution, and the Law on the Sale of Apartments with Tenant's Right of Tenure. The Privatization Agency Law was passed in August 1996. The other three laws had first and second readings in Parliament prior to the September elections; final

---

[13] The Dayton Agreement leaves the Entities responsible for property and privatization issues, inasmuch as it does not assign these responsibilities explicitly to the State level competencies.

passage must be ratified by the new parliament. Other Federation legislation related to privatization includes the Law on Opening Balance Sheets for Enterprises and Banks and the Law on the Privatization of Banks. Drafts of both have been presented to the Federation government.

Table 6.2 Privatizable Enterprises by Canton

Cantons	Total Privatization Candidates [1]	Small Privatization Candidates [2]	Strategic Privatization Candidates [3]	Large Privatization Candidates [4]
Unsko-Sanski	157	50	20	87
Velezupa Posavska	54	11	4	39
Tuzlansko-Podrinski	379	135	35	209
Zenisko-Dobojski	337	157	37	143
Gornjepodrinski	31	11	0	20
Srednobosanski	255	86	33	136
Neretvamjski	253	90	15	148
Zapadno-Herzegovacki	48	14	5	29
Sarajevo	714	300	41	373
Zapadnobosanski	60	18	7	35
TOTAL	2,288	872	197	1,219

1/ Enterprises registered with the Statistics Bureau as having either state, social, or mixed capital.

2/ Enterprises eligible for small scale privatization due to their line of business (sectoral registration) including: transport (road), trade, tourism, catering, and services.

3/ Strategic sectors include: Electricity, transport, water, mining, forest, gambling, banks.

4/ This number is essentially an imperfect residual: total number of privatization candidates, minus small and strategic enterprises.

Together these laws constitute a comprehensive legal framework for the Federation's privatization program. In addition, the Federation government has decided to use privatization to resolve many of the outstanding claims of citizens that had built up prior to and during the war. Settlement will occur when these claims are turned into certificates that can be used to purchase assets being sold by the government through privatization.

The ways in which privatization will be effected in the Federation are described in more detail in the World Bank's Private Sector Assessment for Bosnia and Herzegovina. A few highlights of the settlement mechanism and privatization process are the following:

- Both a Federation Privatization Agency and cantonal privatization agencies are being created. The canton agencies will handle privatization transactions within their cantons, with oversight and under guidelines established by the Federation Agency, which will be responsible also for privatization transactions that involve more than one canton.[14]

- Citizens of the Federation will be given compensation certificates related to four kinds of claims on the state: claims on frozen foreign-exchange deposits; validated restitution claims, where these cannot be settled by restitution of the actual property involved; claims related to unpaid salaries and (possibly) other payment obligations incurred during the war; and a general claim that may be distributed to all citizens, similar to the privatization vouchers used in other transition economies. The amounts of these claims will not be finalized until additional legislation is passed. The certificates issued in compensation for these claims can be used, together with cash, in bids for assets being privatized. The legislation proposes some differentiation among the various certificates for certain transactions (particularly housing). And, for some transactions, a cash component might be required or given preference.

- As in most other transition economies, housing will be preferentially privatized to tenants. This process is more complicated in Bosnia and Herzegovina, however, since tenancy might have changed several times during the war.

- Enterprises are responsible for preparing the initial balance sheets on which privatization transactions will be based. This process includes confirming the extent of privatization that took place under the Marković laws in 1988-90, removing some of the social assets from enterprise books for disposal by the civil authorities, and assessing remaining bank indebtedness, in both local and foreign currencies, to determine how much debt still needs to be dealt with by the enterprise or in accordance with legislative requirements.

- Privatization of medium- and large-sized enterprises will generally be through open auction or sealed tender. Small enterprises will be privatized using open tenders. Additional procedures may be developed for strategic enterprises (see Table 6.2).

The Privatization Agency Law calls for the establishment of the Federal Privatization Agency within 30 days of enactment of the law, and of cantonal agencies within 90 days. The three other basic laws also include timed actions. Based on the provisions in these laws, and assuming enactment of the remaining laws by the end of March 1997, a privatization timetable has been drafted for the Federation (Figure 6.1). Although privatization is off to a good start, any delays or reversals will undermine the government's credibility in the eyes of private investors.

---

[14] Information from the Bureau of Statistics indicate that there are 11 such enterprises: Bosna Auto Sarajevo, Centrotrans Sarajevo, Energoinvest Sarajevo, Magros Sarajevo, RMK Zenica, Soda So Tuzla, Svjetlost Sarajevo, Sipad Sarajevo, Unioninvest Sarajevo, Unis Sarajevo, and UPI Sarajevo.

Figure 6.1 Timetable for the Implementation of Privatization in the Federation

	1997				1998			
	Q1	Q2	Q3	Q4	Q1	Q2	Q3	Q4
Privatization Agencies								
Pass law	▲							
Establish Federal Agency		▲						
Establish Cantonal Agencies		▲						
Develop implementing regulations		▬						
Distribution of Claim Certificates								
Soldiers' back pay	▲							
Frozen foreign exchange deposits			▬▬▬					
General public voucher				▬▬▬▬				
Restitution certificates				▬▬▬▬▬				
Restitution								
Filing of claims			▬▬▬					
Review and settlement of claims				▬▬▬▬▬				
Housing Privatization			▬▬▬▬▬					
Enterprise Privatization								
Prepare initial balance sheets		▬						
Privatize small enterprises		▬▬						
Implement procedures for "strategic" enterprises		▬▬						
Privatize large and strategic enterprises			▬▬▬▬▬▬					

Republika Srpska's privatization plan needs to be rethought

The Law on Privatization of Enterprises of Republika Srpska was adopted in June and published in the Official Gazette on July 8, 1996. The law deals with the privatization of national enterprises, mixed ownership enterprises, and other profit-making judicial persons. Excluded are infrastructure and some undefined strategic enterprises. The basic concept embodied in the law is that the bulk (55 percent) of ownership will be transferred to socially-oriented funds (the shares in these funds would not have voting rights), a further 15 percent will be reserved for cash sale either through the stock exchange or to a strategic investor, and the balance (30 percent) will be sold for vouchers to Republika Srpska citizens using a bidding system somewhat analogous to that used in the Czech and Slovak Republics.

Many of the details of this scheme have yet to be worked out. It is envisaged, for example, that within two years of their inception the funds will distribute their ownership shares to their respective groups of beneficiaries. Who those beneficiaries would be in the case of the Education Fund or the Family Planning Fund is not clear. Meanwhile, Republika Srpska's Privatization Agency is actively trying to undertake valuations of the first 400 or so enterprises to be privatized so that voucher auctions of citizen shares can take place in early 1997. At the same time, arrangements are being made to establish a large number of regional privatization centers to handle these auctions.

Republika Srpska's proposed privatization model has several weaknesses. The current legislation fails to take into account the lessons learned from privatization in other transition economies. In particular:

- The large role envisioned for socially-oriented funds will effectively keep the majority (55 percent) of enterprise shares in the government's hands. Although these shares initially will be nonvoting and will be distributed after two years to the "owners" of the funds, the proposals are so vague that they provide little comfort against the possibility of government interference.

- The relatively minor share (15 percent) proposed for cash sales to strategic investors would not motivate a serious investor, since control would be uncertain. After privatization, the 15 percent stake might motivate the investor to siphon off assets and income.

Both Entities must take the next steps in privatization

The rapid pace at which the rest of the world privatized during Bosnia and Herzegovina's civil war places a high priority and imposes a short time frame on privatization work. Unlike many other countries in the region, Bosnia and Herzegovina's privatization strategy needs to devise appropriate ways of addressing two important issues: identifying viable portions of the large conglomerates that dominated the prewar industrial structure so that they can be rapidly privatized (Box 6.1), and rapidly restoring the essential infrastructure that was severely damaged during the war by promoting the participation of private investors.

Box 6.1 Challenges in Dealing with Large Conglomerates

The main industrial firms in Bosnia and Herzegovina prior to the war were the conglomerates that dominated many industrial sectors and exports. It is estimated that 12 large conglomerates produced about 35 percent of GDP, while 4 of these firms accounted for some 40 percent of exports in the prewar period. These large, sprawling enterprises were often vertically integrated in all phases of production and distribution (e.g., they produced many of their intermediate inputs, owned their own trucking fleets, etc.) and horizontally branched out into completely unrelated sectors. Many of these firms supplied the military complex of the former Soviet Union and developing countries. Therefore, they have lost most of their customer base and seen most of their marketing and distribution channels thoroughly disrupted. The experiences of other economies have shown that such large conglomerates have generally not been viable in a competitive, market-oriented economy. In other countries, such conglomerates have been broken up and their viable subcomponents have been spun off and privatized.

In Bosnia and Herzegovina, the normal problems of dealing with such conglomerates are complicated by the fact that they were heavily damaged during the war, and their assets and activities, which are centered around just five cities (Bihać, Mostar, Sarajevo, Tuzla, and Zenica), have been split between the Entities. It is likely that many conglomerate activities are no longer viable. Major structural changes in the economies of trading partners mean that the demand for some conglomerate outputs has diminished; price distortions that prevailed prior to the war and were the key to the viability of some conglomerate activities are no longer there or are being removed; and, similarly, subsidies and trade protection that were essential to the viability of some activities have been phased out.

The challenge in Bosnia and Herzegovina will be for each Entity to identify those portions of conglomerates which are salvageable (i.e., activities for which markets exist and investors can be found) and to move them as quickly as possible into the private sector. This might entail changing laws, clarifying investment regulations, and having realistic expectations in terms of what the newly-privatized companies will produce and how much employment they will generate, especially in the short term. Care must be taken, moreover, to ensure that no monopolies are created or maintained and that investment incentives do not include such "sweeteners" as guaranteed market share or protective tariffs.

Like many reforms, privatization will proceed on parallel tracks in the two Entities. In the Federation this approach will require focused, committed progress on:

- Implementing of the 1996 Privatization Agency Law and ratifying and implementing the Law on the Privatization of Enterprises, Law on Restitution, and the Law on the Sale of Apartments with Tenant's Right of Tenure;

- Creating the federal and cantonal privatization agencies;

- Enacting and implementing other legislation related to opening balance sheets for enterprises and banks, and finalizing proposals to distribute compensatory certificates to citizens for frozen foreign-exchange accounts, restitution, salary claims, and general claims;

- Privatizing housing, with preference for tenants, and enterprises, through open auction, sealed bid, or special procedure; and

- Opening infrastructure investment and management to competition (where appropriate) and private participation (everywhere).

Similar measures need to be adopted in Republika Srpska to supplement or correct the current provisions of the Law on the Privatization of Enterprises. These measures should increase the portion of enterprise shares to be privatized, make privatization more transparent, and encourage foreign investment.

The Business Environment Needs To Be Improved

In addition to managing privatization, the government must move steadily to develop an effective legal and regulatory framework to support private-sector development. Bosnia and Herzegovina shares with the other republics of former Yugoslavia the institutional legacy of heavy regulation of economic activity. These controls were embedded in the legal and regulatory framework. Other transition economies have recognized that their legal and institutional frameworks required major overhaul in order to support a private sector-led market economy.[15] Here again, the structural problems inherent in the Yugoslav framework were exacerbated by the war. Three areas require immediate progress: reintegrating or harmonizing laws throughout the country, reforming and strengthening private property rights, and rationalizing taxes and tax administration.

Compatible laws are essential

During the war, the de facto partition of the country into three ethnically based regimes led to the development of similar but distinct legal regimes in the Bosniac-majority areas, Croat-majority areas, and Republika Srpska. The first two areas are formally unified as the Federation. This unification required dissolution of the so-called Herzeg-Bosna Croat "mini-state," including

---

[15] However, the Yugoslav variant of socialism was less centralized than that in most other economies, and private economic activity always existed in the law and in practice.

all institutions, laws, and regulations, and is in train. In addition, legislation from the former Yugoslavia is still in place where no new legislation has replaced it. The Entities are now issuing legislation, as is the new State government. This multitude of sources of legislation results in a confusing and conflicting legal framework for businesses and substantially diminishes the protective and stabilizing influence of the law.

Private property rights must be strengthened

Problems with private property rights are particularly acute. Clear and secure private property rights are needed to provide entrepreneurs with the incentive to invest and to obtain secured financing. The Yugoslav legal system accorded weak protection to such rights and the pursuit of war-related goals led to widespread nationalization, expropriation, and centralization over the past five years, further undermining security of private property. The expansion of administrative control over the economy and property occurred throughout the country, but was most extensive in the Bosniac- and Serb-majority areas. This nationalization largely ignored the property rights of shareholders who had received their shares under the Marković privatization program. Private commercial and residential property and tenure rights have been expropriated following forced and voluntary departures of citizens. Though much of this expropriation is officially temporary, there has been little progress in restoring property anywhere in Bosnia and Herzegovina. The authorities must also move to fill in the gaps of the legal system, which often block market development in reforming economies. For example, the absence of a functioning framework for bankruptcy, providing a clear basis for secured lending and creditor priority, must be addressed.[16]

Both the Federation Constitution and the Constitution of Republika Srpska provide for broader protection of private property rights and recognize a wider range of activities for private enterprises. Though both Entities are moving to undertake systemic reforms and to amend the socialist and labor-management legacy inherited by all the republics of former Yugoslavia, progress is uneven. The Federation is further ahead in promulgating or amending the legislation needed for transition, including a much improved Enterprise Law.

As in most other transition economies, there is a need to strike a better balance between a strong state to enforce laws and impose order and constraints on state power to allow for the emergence of strong individual rights. This task has been complicated by the legacy of the war. Throughout the country, the judicial system has been severely weakened, often to the point of disintegration. Thus, in addition to changes in the laws, the role of the constitutional courts must be strengthened and the commercial court system must be reinvigorated to provide for effective interpretation, dissemination, and enforcement of new laws and regulations. It will be equally important to support the development of informal institutions that promote information flows and monitor the government and market participants. Accountants, credit rating services, securities regulators, and an independent media play a crucial role in the development of the rule of law.

---

[16] The current law--the 1985 former Yugoslavia Law on Bankruptcy, Compulsory Settlement, and Liquidation of Enterprises--provides only for a reorganization of a company with excess labor.

Tax structures should be rationalized

Most enterprises view the rationalization of taxes and duties, and of the administrative requirements associated with them, as the most urgently needed reform. The existing structure of official fees and procedures places a heavy burden on businesses in terms of the monetary and time costs required for compliance. It also has encouraged the development of a large informal economy that law-abiding enterprises regard as unfair competition. Rectifying these weaknesses is essential to building respect for the law and to boosting the government's ability to regulate markets and collect revenues.

The Dayton Agreement formed the basis for dual sources of legislation: the State, governing trade, customs, monetary policy, and international agreements; and the Entities, governing those areas not explicitly assigned to the State. Since the bulk of the legal framework for economic activity will be under Entity authority—including property law, contract law, competition law, labor law, and a substantial portion of domestic trade and tax laws—progress on legal and regulatory reform at the Entity level is essential. The following actions are needed:

- Unifying the legal systems in the Federation and harmonizing Entity-level legal frameworks;

- Lowering the cost of transactions by reducing tax, fee, and regulatory requirements associated with business entry, sales, and contracting;

- Improving information flows by publishing all relevant laws and regulations and enforcing international accounting standards for banks and enterprises;

- Establishing a fair and transparent system of property rights, both in basic property law and in laws on privatization and restitution;

- Updating contract and enterprise laws to remove discretion and provide a coherent basis for private ownership;

- Drafting banking laws that provide the basis for effective collateral and registration of property;

- Upgrading and retraining the judiciary, and reforming the means for appointing, compensating, and removing judges;

- Creating a clear legal basis for bankruptcy and liquidation, training a professional cadre of trustees, and developing a commercial arbitration system; and

- Introducing or strengthening the legal basis for corporate governance, regulation of competition, and securities.

Chapter VII

Restructuring and Privatizing the Banking Sector

Of the 53 banks in Bosnia and Herzegovina, 42 are licensed to operate in the Federation and 11 are in Republika Srpska. Most banks are very small on a stock balance-sheet basis, with very few active loans, negligible levels of active deposits, and limited or negative capital. In mid-1996, prior to writeoffs, these banks held an average of DM 162 million in assets and DM 10 million in capital. However, it is widely assumed that about 90 percent of the assets of the old banks (those that existed prior to independence) are nonperforming and immobile. Thus, after writeoffs, banks held an average of DM 21 million in assets, and capital for the largest banks is deeply negative.

The main components of socially- and State-owned banks' balance sheets are: about DM 4 billion in household foreign-currency deposits (on the liability side) and corresponding claims (nonperforming assets) on the former National Bank of Yugoslavia that have no present value;[17] about DM 3 to 4.5 billion in foreign-currency borrowings from international creditors that the banks lent to state enterprises (nonperforming assets), which were often the banks' owners, to finance projects;[18] and about DM 1 billion in other assets and liabilities, mostly denominated in local currency, that lost value as a result of hyperinflation in 1992-93 and the collapse of economic activity.

The small size of Bosnia and Herzegovina's banks reflects limited financial capacity and low levels of financial intermediation at a time when lending and investment resources are critically needed for recovery. Thus, reform efforts need to focus on increasing private investment into the banking sector, introducing new governance and management structures to provide for safe and sound banks, and restoring depositor confidence so that banks have the resources to provide sufficient levels of intermediation for economic growth.

Banks that existed before independence are generally hobbled by immobile and nonperforming assets due to their exposure to enterprises that are now technically bankrupt. Banks that were created after independence are small, have limited experience with managing credit and mobilizing deposits, and often are set up to lend back to shareholders. In both types of banks, management capacity is limited, governance is weak, and commercial risk management practices have not yet been institutionalized. Moreover, neither class of banks is strong enough

---

[17] The National Bank of Yugoslavia extended equivalent amounts of credits in Yugoslav dinars to domestic banks that had placed foreign-exchange deposits with it and used the foreign exchange to repay the Federal Republic of Yugoslavia's foreign debts and finance imports by enterprises. Most of these dinar credits were not repaid.

[18] These projects can no longer be continued because of the war and the almost complete halting of production in some parts of Bosnia and Herzegovina. Many assets have been physically damaged or destroyed. Loans extended to enterprises to finance such projects are nonperforming and can only be classified as losses.

financially or operationally to restore public confidence in the banking system. Nor do these banks operate according to the incentive structures (for example, limiting exposure to shareholders and avoiding connected lending) that are needed to transform the system into one that is transparent, accountable, and market-driven. Only a handful of banks show promise and are moving in this direction.

Meanwhile, pervasive uncertainty on issues related to the settlement of displaced persons, dispute resolution, and general economic recovery limit the resources people are willing to deposit in banks. Mobilizing deposits would be challenging enough given the freezing of foreign currency accounts in 1992. But pervasive uncertainty that exists today compounds the challenge, making it more difficult for banks to obtain the low-cost funding base needed to raise intermediation levels to the point needed for economic recovery. Until confidence is restored, banks will continue to contribute only marginally to reconstruction.

Several reforms are needed to restore lenders' and investors' confidence. Some have already been introduced, and work on many others is underway. These include:

- Restructuring and privatizing banks in a way that attracts strategic investment, changes ownership and governance structures, and leads to a new approach to management consistent with new laws and regulations;

- Supporting the development of private banks in a way that is consistent with safe and sound banking principles in a market economy; and

- Changing the legal and regulatory framework to provide incentives and an enabling environment for banks to take risk and to prudently manage that risk, for enterprises to properly manage their resources (including bank debt), and for disputes to be adjudicated fairly and promptly in a way that enforces contract terms and protects property rights.

Banking Sector is Insolvent and Dominated by Social Ownership

On a stock basis, total banking system assets were DM 8.6 billion (nearly US$6 billion) in mid-1996. But with an estimated 90 percent of assets considered immobile or nonperforming, banking system assets are more likely to have been about DM 1.1 billion,[19] or an average of DM 21 million per bank. After assumed writeoffs, even the largest banks are likely to have no more than DM 135 million (US$90 million) in assets. By comparison, the largest banks in countries in the OECD tend to have tens of billions of dollars in assets on their balance sheets, and capital equal to about 8 percent of assets (on a risk-weighted basis).

Banking system capital is said to be DM 542 million (about US$361 million), although it is widely recognized that aggregate capital is actually negative due to writeoffs that have not yet been made. Writeoffs are at least DM 3.6 billion (US$2.4 billion),[20] far in excess of the capital held by the banking system. If the 90 percent estimate of writeoffs is accurate for the 42 or so banks that had reported to the NBBH and NBRS by June 30, 1996,[21] aggregate bank insolvency is about DM 6.9 billion (134 percent of 1996 GDP).[22]

In terms of flows, banks are doing fairly well in generating fee income. In recent years banks have generated profits by engaging in transfer services and other fee-generating activities. These earnings have eased some banks' liquidity constraints and contributed to capital growth.

---

[19] Federation banks reporting to the National Bank of Bosnia and Herzegovina in Sarajevo on June 30, 1996, showed nearly DM 6.2 billion in assets. Republika Srpska banks reporting to the National Bank of Republika Srpska in Banja Luka on May 31, 1996, showed nearly DM 2.1 billion in assets. However, Federation banks reporting to the local authorities in Mostar on June 30, 1996, showed only DM 338 million in assets. Thus it appears that the Mostar-based banks have already written off a significant portion of their immobile assets, while the other two regions appear to be carrying the old values. If those values are discounted about 90 percent and added to the DM 270 million in assets of the Mostar-based banks (total assets net of some dubious long-term resources, reserves and an insurance fund for one heavily damaged bank), total banking system assets in Bosnia and Herzegovina are DM 1,092 million, or about US$728 million.

[20] The National Bank of Bosnia and Herzegovina in Sarajevo showed "potential losses" that could be written off against capital to be DM 1,969,837 for banks reporting to it in June 1996. Meanwhile, National Bank of Republika Srpska figures from Banja Luka show that household deposits (which are mostly frozen) and long-term loans (which are mostly nonperforming rollovers) were DM 1,615,403 as of May 31, 1996. Balance sheet figures for Mostar-based banks only showed capital, insurance and reserves; these data do not explicitly reveal the value of potential losses or writeoffs, although these may have already been made by the banks that existed prior to independence, as reflected in their far smaller nominal balance-sheet values.

[21] About 20 percent of assets are assumed to be nonperforming among the banks that reported to the Ministry of Finance in Mostar in mid-1996.

[22] A 90 percent writeoff of assets in the 42 banks that reported to the National Bank of Bosnia and Herzegovina in Sarajevo and the National Bank of Republika Srpska Banja Luka in mid-1996 is about DM 7.4 billion (US$4.9 billion). Capital for these banks totals DM 542 million (US$361 million). The net is about DM 6.9 billion.

However, most of the fee-generating services carried out by banks in market economies (underwriting, financial advisory services, custodial functions, cash management) are absent in Bosnia and Herzegovina. Trade finance services have resumed somewhat as reconstruction has gotten under way. Still the income stream from these activities is small; retained earnings from these activities will not allow banks to significantly improve their negative capital positions.

Meanwhile, banks are generally unwilling to assume balance-sheet risk. Most banks have no more than 20 or 30 active loans on which they are taking risk, and these are usually short-term trade-related transactions. Although interest rates are high (about 2 percent a month for loans, with higher rates for nonlending services), the volume of activity is insufficient for banks to achieve the levels of capitalization needed for lending and investment. A cursory balance-sheet profile of the banking system, based on ownership, is shown in Table 7.1.

Table 7.1 Profile of Bosnia and Herzegovina's Banking System, 1996*

(DM '000)	Bosniac-Majority Areas (NBBH)	Croat-Majority Areas	NBRS	Total
No. of Banks	33	9	11	53
o/w nonprivate	15	0	8	23
o/w private	18	9	3	30
Assets	6,154,959	337,548	2,069,653	8,562,160
o/w nonprivate	6,108,591	0	2,041,564	8,150,155
o/w private	46,368	337,548	28,089	412,005
Loans	n.a.	91,159	408,451	n.a.
o/w nonprivate	n.a.	0	393,839	n.a.
o/w private	n.a.	91,159	14,612	n.a.
Deposits**	n.a.	n.a.	1,323,114	n.a.
o/w nonprivate	n.a.	n.a.	1,318,960	n.a.
o/w private	n.a.	n.a.	4,154	n.a.
Capital	350,104	46,363	145,208	541,675
o/w nonprivate	321,286	0	132,752	454,038
o/w private	28,818	46,363	12,456	87,637
Net Capital	(1,622,319)	24,748	n.a.	n.a.
o/w nonprivate	(1,649,232)	0	n.a.	n.a.
o/w private	26,913	24,748	n.a.	n.a.

* *Note*: Figures are through the first half of 1996, prior to the formation of the Federal Banking Agency in the Federation. Therefore, banks are grouped by authorities to which they reported. Totals are aggregated. Figures for the NBBH region are for June 30, 1996 except for assets, which are for December 31, 1995. Figures for the Mostar region are for June 30, 1996. Figures for banks in Republika Srpska are for May 31, 1996. Figures in the Federation were expressed in DM. Figures from Republika Srpska were converted from FRY dinar to DM at a 3.47:1 rate.

** *Note*: Based on the monetary survey prepared in April 1996, deposits net of State and Entity government deposits were estimated to be DM 325.9 million in the Federation and DM 210.2 million in Republika Srpska. Federation figures exclude frozen foreign-exchange accounts, which are included in Republika Srpska's banks' figures.

Sources: Federal Banking Agency; National Bank of Bosnia and Herzegovina (Sarajevo); National Bank of Republika Srpska(Banja Luka); World Bank; IMF.

Assets are concentrated in a few weak nonprivate banks

Balance-sheet figures prior to writeoffs show a high degree of concentration in a few socially- or State-owned banks. The 23 nonprivate banks account for 95 percent of total assets, with 6 accounting for 79 percent.[23] About 76 percent of nominal asset values are held by the 42 banks in the Federation, and 24 percent are with the 11 banks in Republika Srpska.

These large banks (prior to writeoffs) were the key national banks in the former Yugoslavia, dealing with international creditors and financing public enterprises, wholesale trade, and large-scale projects. However, after writeoffs, these banks have small balance sheets, and they are differentiated from their competitors only by the roles they played in the former Yugoslavia. Today, they are shells of their former organizational structures, with fewer employees, lost branches, inter-Entity and cross-border claims, and exposure to enterprises that are technically bankrupt.

The ownership structure is mixed

Of the 53 banks, 30 are majority private(mainly in the Federation) and 23 are majority or wholly nonprivate. Socially- and State-owned banks predominate in Republika Srpska and are still influential in part of the Federation. Private banks are showing increasing market presence in the Federation, although their resource base remains very small. Private banks have had little or no impact in Republika Srpska, and the three that exist are managed and operated much like State banks.

The 23 nonprivate banks have varying sizes and locations, with 15 in the Federation and 8 in Republika Srpska. Most are mid-sized by Bosnia and Herzegovina standards, and serve a specific regional market. They also tend to have mixed ownership, although private shareholdings are minority stakes and partial privatization has not led to new injections of capital. Many of these banks were spun off from Privredna Bank in 1989-90. A few larger banks (Privredna-Sarajevo, Union Bank, Banja Luka Banka, Privredna-Doboj) reflect the past emphasis on large-scale industrial projects, international transactions, and enterprise deposit mobilization. These banks are the most financially troubled, as they carry the bulk of nonperforming assets from the former Yugoslavia. Nonprivate banks account for 95 percent of asset values prior to writeoffs, and more than 60 percent after writeoffs.[24] However, unlike most of the smaller banks, the capital positions of the largest socially- and State-owned banks are negative.

Since 1991, 30 majority-private banks have been established. In some cases, those are former socially-owned banks that have been privatized by transforming ownership (such as Hrvatska Bank) rather than by attracting meaningful levels of new private investment. Most of the private banks are small banks that were founded during the war to handle international

---

[23]   These banks are Privredna-Sarajevo and Union in the Federation and Banja Luka Banka, Privredna-Doboj, Jugobanka and Prijedorska in Republika Srpska. Together they account for DM 6.8 billion in book-valued assets, or 79 percent of the total DM 8.6 billion.

[24]   After writeoffs, nonprivate banks' assets are estimated to be about DM 680 million. Estimated values of aggregate banking system assets after writeoffs are nearly DM 1.1 billion.

transfers. They have limited capital and almost no experience with lending or deposit mobilization. In the Federation, 27 private banks hold assets totaling DM 384 million (US$256 million). Republika Srpska's three private banks hold only DM 28 million (US$19 million) in assets. On a stock basis, the private banks hold about 5 percent of nominal balance-sheet values. But, if nonperforming assets were excluded from nonprivate banks' balance sheets, the private banks' asset values would account for nearly 40 percent of the total.[25]

Balance sheets are weak

Prior to writeoffs, two Federation banks (Privredna-Sarajevo and Union) reporting to the NBBH in Sarajevo accounted for DM 5.1 billion in assets—59 percent of the total for all banks in Bosnia and Herzegovina in mid-1996, and 82.5 percent of the total among banks reporting to the National Bank at the end of 1995.[26] Among banks that reported to the Ministry of Finance in Mostar in mid-1996, two (Hrvatska and Livno) accounted for 78 percent of resources.[27] In Republika Srpska, four banks (Banja Luka Banka, Privredna-Doboj, Jugobanka, and Prijedorska) accounted for DM 1.7 billion in assets in mid-1996, 20 percent of the total for all banks in Bosnia and Herzegovina, and 82 percent of the total among banks reporting to the NBRS. Thus, prior to writeoffs, eight banks accounted for about 80 percent of total banking system assets, with high levels of regional concentration.

Most of these banks are large socially- and State-owned banks that operated throughout much of the former Yugoslavia. Privredna was active in both Entities and beyond, focusing on public enterprises; until the 1989-90 reorganization, 11 of the 53 banks in Bosnia and Herzegovina today were part of the Privredna network.[28] Together, prior to writeoffs, these banks accounted for 64 percent of total banking-system assets in mid-1996.[29] Union Bank

---

[25] Private banks' assets are valued at about DM 412 million. Estimated values of aggregate banking system assets after writeoffs are nearly DM 1.1 billion.

[26] Privredna posted DM 3.6 billion in assets, 59 percent of NBBH banks' totals and 42 percent of aggregated assets for all of Bosnia and Herzegovina banks in mid-1996. Union posted assets of DM 1.5 billion, 24 percent of NBBH banks' totals and 17 percent of aggregated assets for all of Bosnia and Herzegovina banks in mid-1996. Asset figures for banks reporting to NBBH are for end 1995.

[27] Hrvatska Bank and Livno Bank reported far lower asset figures in mid-1996 of DM 163 million and DM 100 million, respectively. However, these were 78 percent of asset values among banks reporting to the Ministry of Finance in Mostar at the time. (Since then, the Federal Banking Agency has been established, and all banks licensed to operate on Federation territory report to the Agency.) The lower values for Hrvatska Bank are presumed to reflect writeoffs, giving it a larger profile in Bosnia and Herzegovina on an asset basis after assumed writeoffs. However, 70 percent of Livno Bank's balance sheet is composed of "other assets," and, therefore, it is not considered to be a major bank.

[28] These banks are Central Bank, Privredna-Sarajevo, Privredna-Travnik, Privredna-Bihać, Banja Luka Banka, Privredna-Doboj, Privredna-Pale, Privredna-Brcko, Privredna-Gradiska, Gospodarska-Mostar, and Livno Bank.

[29] Total assets were DM 5.5 billion of a total DM 8.6 billion. This does not include assets from Privredna in Bihać.

(in the Federation) and Jugobanka (in Republika Srpska) were both part of the larger Jugobanka system active throughout former Yugoslavia. At mid-1996, the combined resources of these banks approximated 22 percent of total system assets in Bosnia and Herzegovina.[30] Hrvatska Bank and Livno Bank, the two largest banks in the southwestern region of Bosnia and Herzegovina, deviate from this pattern. These banks have far smaller balance sheets than the others; Hrvatska was not tied to the Privredna or Jugobanka systems, but was linked with Croatian banks. Their stocks of nonperforming loans are much smaller than those in the other large banks, although the biggest item on Livno Bank's balance sheet is "other assets," largely financed by questionable "long-term resources."

In general, the large socially- and State-owned banks have had more exposure to large transactions and represent larger markets than the banks that have been established in recent years. But, the large banks face a major writedown of asset values because of three broad asset categories: claims on the former National Bank of Yugoslavia for foreign-currency deposits, estimated at DM 4 billion; claims on enterprises for hard currency loans that originated with international financial institutions and Paris and London Club creditors, estimated at DM 3 billion; and local currency-denominated assets that have lost value because of hyperinflation and the effects of the war, estimated at DM 1 billion. In the Federation almost all

Table 7.2 Estimated Impact of Writeoffs on the Banking System

DM '000	NBBH	Croat-Major. Areas	NBRS	Total
Assets Before Writeoffs*	6,154,959	337,548	2,069,653	8,562,160
Average per Bank	186,514	37,505	188,150	161,550
Capital Before Writeoffs	350,104	46,363	145,208	541,675
Average per Bank	10,609	5,151	13,201	10,220
Assets After Writeoffs**	615,496	269,831	206,965	1,092,292
Average per Bank	18,651	29,981	18,815	20,609
Capital After Writeoffs	(5,189,359)	(21,354)	(1,717,480)	(6,928,193)
Average per Bank	(157,253)	(2,373)	(156,135)	(130,721)

* *Note*: Pre-writeoff figures are through the first half of 1996, prior to the formation of the Federal Banking Agency in the Federation. Therefore, banks are grouped by authorities to which they reported. Totals are aggregated. Figures for the NBBH region are for June 30, 1996 except for assets, which are for December 31, 1995. Figures for Mostar region are for June 30, 1996. Figures for banks in Republika Srpska are for May 31, 1996. Figures in the Federation were expressed in DM. Figures from Republika Srpska were converted from FRY dinar to DM at a 3.47:1 rate.

** *Note*: Assumptions for writeoffs are 90 percent for NBBH banks and banks in Republika Srpska. Banks reporting in mid-1996 in Mostar are assumed to have written off most nonperforming and immobile assets. Subtracted from reported asset values are long-term resources for Livno Bank, the insurance fund for Gospodarska-Mostar, and the minimal reserves held by the 11 banks. These writeoffs are all subtracted from capital figures, and amount to about 20 percent of assets.

Sources: Federal Banking Agency; National Bank of Bosnia and Herzegovina (Sarajevo); National Bank of Republika Srpska (Banja Luka); World Bank estimates.

---

[30]   Total assets were DM 1.9 billion of a total DM 8.6 billion, about 80 percent of which was with Union Bank in Sarajevo and another 20 percent with Jugobanka in Republika Srpska.

of these values are held with Privredna-Sarajevo and Union Bank. Although other banks hold frozen foreign-currency deposits and local currency-denominated assets that lost value, Privredna holds 80 percent of Federation bank exposure to international financial institutions and Paris and London Club creditors; Union Bank holds the remaining 20 percent. In Republika Srpska almost all of these assets are held by the remnants of the Privredna system, mainly Banja Luka Banka and Privredna Doboj; Prijedorska Banka also has significant exposure to international creditors. Along with the various Privredna banks, Jugobanka and Prijedorska Banka also have large claims on the former National Bank of Yugoslavia for frozen foreign-currency deposits.

The structure of the banking system changes dramatically once writeoffs are taken into account. Rather than having eight large banks dominating the market, the banking environment is characterized by small banks with varying forms of ownership operating in fragmented markets. If claims on the former National Bank of Yugoslavia and foreign-currency loans are removed from the balance sheets of the larger banks, along with their corresponding liabilities and capital, the banks have negative or very limited capital (Table 7.2)

Restructuring and Privatizing Banks

To restore public confidence in the banking system and establish the conditions for banks to provide needed intermediation and related services, banking-sector reform will need to focus on: the rapid restructuring and privatization of banks, with the goal of attracting strategic investment to provide needed capital, creating new ownership and governance structures, and developing the management skills needed for competitive banks in a market economy; maintaining openness to the entry of private banks, consistent with new licensing and supervisory requirements dedicated to safe and sound banking principles; and changing the legal and regulatory framework to provide incentives and an enabling environment for banks to compete and take risk in support of larger efforts to stimulate investment in the economy.

Restructuring and privatizing socially- and State-owned banks

Although many private banks have been established in recent years, most banks remain wholly or majority socially or State owned. Still, most banks that are not yet private expect to be privatized at some point. Most anticipate that some type of ownership transformation will take place; as the enterprise owners of the banks become private, the banks will follow. The problem with this approach is that it fails to attract new capital to a severely undercapitalized banking system, and it provides no guarantee that the new "private" owners will exercise better governance and oversight.

Restructuring and privatizing socially-owned banks is essential if Bosnia and Herzegovina is to develop a market economy, and if its banking sector is to follow commercial practices in accordance with prudent guidelines. The goal is to attract strategic investment— focused on turning around existing banks or establishing new banks able to provide intermediation and services—as a vehicle to accelerate bank privatization and reform, and to inject capital into a system that is about DM 7 billion insolvent (140 percent of 1996 GDP). An aggressive bank privatization program is also needed to clean up troubled banks' balance sheets in a period of limited fiscal resources, and to adjust ownership and incentive structures to make them compatible with a market economy. Large socially-owned banks with experienced staff and management can only be expected to perform if they write off nonperforming assets against capital and reserves, find new owners (without insider or connected access to easy loans that they fail to service or repay) who introduce better management practices and accounting systems, and are forced to compete.

Privatization is likely to involve several approaches based on each bank's prospects for attracting strategic investment from domestic or foreign sources, merging with other banks, and liquidating parts that are not salvageable. Large socially- and State-owned banks are likely to be most affected by the program, since they have the most severe financial problems. At the same time, some of these banks have qualified staff, long-standing relations with foreign markets, and management eager to introduce private sector-oriented practices in an open, competitive market economy. The second tier of nonprivate banks, with a focus on local markets but unburdened by nonperforming loans, is likely to be targeted to expand market coverage and branch networks. Private banks are also likely to be joint venture partners for foreign banks with long-term intentions of investing in Bosnia and Herzegovina.

Privatization will likely be complicated by two impediments. Country risk is first and foremost, and will not abate until progress is made on the resettlement of citizens and refugees and the settlement of disputes. Private investment will not materialize until these obstacles are removed. For this reason it is critical that the authorities resolve outstanding issues promptly and fairly. Although less problematic, a second impediment to rapid privatization is the size of Bosnia and Herzegovina's market. Still, countries with smaller populations have attracted significant investment in the banking sector when stability has prevailed, an enabling environment has been put in place, and incomes and purchasing power have risen.[31] Thus, success with bank privatization is closely linked to improvements in the overall economy.

As part of the privatization of banks, and in some instances, as preconditions to privatization, balance sheets will be restructured. Restructuring is likely to involve netting out claims and severing enterprise ownership of insolvent banks; cleaning up troubled banks' balance sheets, including transferring nonperforming assets, foreign-currency deposits, and other foreign-currency liabilities to a government agency; and changing boards and management, credit policies and procedures, internal and external reporting practices, and other areas to bring troubled banks to the point where they can be profitable and privatized. The netting out of claims will serve as the starting point for severing the ownership ties of delinquent or bankrupt enterprises. Banks will then be able to adopt a more commercial orientation. While assets and liabilities will be transferred from bank balance sheets to a government agency, banks' claims on enterprises will not be released until these enterprises are privatized. This approach will shrink bank and enterprise balance sheets to more realistic levels, but will require that they be privatized with the objective of obtaining strategic investment.

The assets and liabilities to be transferred from bank balance sheets are estimated to be about DM 7-8 billion on a book valued basis. A government agency needs to be set up to handle international negotiations pertaining to these assets (such as succession negotiations with Yugoslavia for outstanding claims on the former National Bank of Yugoslavia, loans made to enterprises by banks on the basis of credits from external creditors, and loans made with former

---

[31]   Slovenia has the highest purchasing power of any transition economy, but contains only 2 million people. Nevertheless, it has attracted significant investment in the financial sector from neighboring countries because it has stabilized its economy and established an enabling environment for investors.

government guarantees) and to handle claims on banks (such as the DM 4 billion in frozen foreign-currency deposits and DM 3 billion in international creditors' claims on banks). This agency also should establish and implement policies, procedures, and mechanisms to resolve and liquidate claims.

Resolution of claims is expected to involve the privatization of enterprises and public housing, although this process has not yet begun. However, first steps have been taken, with preparation in the Federation of privatization laws, plans for the establishment of the Federal Privatization Agency, and drafting of legislation related to balance-sheet restructuring and bank privatization. Final legislation will need to be passed promptly, and Republika Srpska will need to accelerate its move toward legal reform in these areas in a way that is harmonized with Federation legislation. Inter-Entity working groups are making progress in this area.

Technical assistance, including customized twinning arrangements, is to be utilized as a tool to accelerate bank privatization. Plans for bank privatizations should be designed to secure strategic investment as quickly as possible. These plans will need to provide details on:

- Anticipated market focus (area services);

- Projected financial performance (based on the bank's new strategy);

- How objectives will be achieved (through consolidation with other banks, acquisition of other banks' branches or operations, sale of properties and other assets to restructure the balance sheet and increase cash resources);

- Which new governance and management systems will be introduced and how they will operate (taking into account new laws and regulations);

- What operating systems, procedures, and controls will be used to implement the plan;

- How, when, and from whom the bank expects to attract strategic investment; and

- How to solicit foreign investment in the banks.

Supporting and strengthening private banks

As noted, more than 30 private banks have emerged in Bosnia and Herzegovina in the past several years. Most are small, with less than DM 2.5 million in net capital and limited experience. However, as elsewhere in Central Europe, many of these banks have generated considerable fee income from transfers and remittances, trade finance, foreign-exchange trading, and other off-balance-sheet activities. While these activities are not sufficient to develop the economy, some of these banks possess the building blocks for future development and growth. Further, they are unburdened by the loan problems that hamper the socially-owned banks in both Entities.

Technical assistance will be needed to strengthen private banks' policies, procedures, management, and systems. Such assistance will be modeled on successful line of credit programs already in place. These banks will also be encouraged to merge with other banks to build branch networks, broaden their potential deposit bases, tap into other markets for good credit prospects, boost capital, and expand management capacity. Consolidation should provide mid-sized banks of mixed ownership with an incentive to privatize quickly, particularly since their financial condition does not require complex restructuring.

Improving the legal, regulatory, and institutional environment

Improvements in the legal, regulatory, and institutional environment are essential to developing a competitive economy and a market-based banking system. These improvements should include:

- Adopting legislation to establish the State Central Bank and an independent Banking Supervision Agency in Republika Srpska, lay out commercial banking guidelines in both Entities, provide the supervisory agencies of both Entities with a mandate to enforce regulations, and produce the initial body of legislation required to address weaknesses in both Entities' collateral, mortgage, bankruptcy, insurance, and capital markets laws;

- Introducing new banking-sector regulations and building institutional capacity to enforce prudential regulations in support of a safe and sound banking system, including new rules on connected lending, related-party lending, loan classification, loan concentration, and exposure limits; and

- Introducing a new accounting framework in concert with new regulations to generate more meaningful financial data for a market-based economy, facilitate bank supervision, and enhance financial disclosure for shareholders, depositors, and consumers.

These improvements will require continued coordination between the working groups from both Entities, until the main elements of an enabling environment for the financial sector are in place for the entire country.

Although progress has been made on certain laws, little effort has been made to establish a regulatory framework that provides clear and practical guidelines for bank supervision. Bank supervision traditionally has been passive, and only now is beginning to address issues of systemic risk. Moreover, these efforts are only occurring in the Federation; they have yet to occur in Republika Srpska. In addition to developing appropriate legislation and fostering independent, well-staffed supervisory agencies able to conduct onsite inspections as well as offsite surveillance, both Entities need: a harmonized prudential regulatory framework that details licensing standards, (including minimum capital requirements, scope of operations, shareholder and management requirements, and reporting requirements); capital adequacy standards that properly reflect risk management safeguards; loan classification systems that reflect proper risk weights and account for delinquencies and interest capitalization; loan concentration restrictions to large borrowers and insiders; foreign-exchange operations and exposure to contain systemic risk; and credit policy and procedures to enhance the prospects for successful credit management. Some progress has been made since the September 1996 elections and with the establishment of the Federal Banking Agency, but more effort is needed to accelerate the development of active bank supervision with recognized licensing and enforcement powers. Progress is expected as new laws and regulations come into place, and as the respective supervisory agencies introduce new systems and procedures for offsite surveillance, onsite inspections, and other examination techniques.

These efforts will have to include a new accounting framework based on international standards, including more open disclosure for regulators, depositors, and investors. New accounting standards will be needed not only for banks, but also for enterprises. These standards will have to be consistent with new laws and regulations, and reflect incentives that encourage prudent resource management in a competitive environment. To foster institutional development, a domestic auditing profession will need to be developed.

Main Issues and Challenges in the Medium Term

Once the basic laws and institutions are in place, banks and the authorities will have to confront a number of remaining challenges: restoring public confidence in banks, changing incentive systems and bank cultures, providing compensation for frozen foreign-currency assets, building the weak deposit base, unifying the payments system, strengthening asset and risk management, and clarifying the role of nonbank financial institutions.

Restoring public confidence. Bosnia and Herzegovina's banking system suffers from a lack of depositor confidence in its safety and soundness, a low level of financial intermediation, and a limited range of banking services. These weaknesses limit the sources of funding available to banks, constraining the provision of credit. The scarcity of resources is also partly due to the low quality of assets, with poor credit management impairing banks' liquidity and solvency and raising the cost of credit. Combined, these undermine prospects for economic growth and recovery. A key medium-term goal must be to restore confidence in the system.

Changing incentives and bank culture. Banks that existed before the war are generally hobbled by immobile and nonperforming assets due to their exposure to enterprises that are now technically bankrupt. In many cases these enterprises were the owners of the banks, reflecting the noncommercial orientation of a banking system that relied on connected lending, excess concentration, distorted classifications, and the passive administrative role banks played in disbursing credits to their owners. The poor quality of these banks' loan portfolios (and the associated incentive structure) is the main cause of their technical insolvency. These factors, combined with the freezing of foreign-currency accounts by the former Yugoslavia, make it difficult to restore public confidence in these banks. Nothing less than a full-scale change in incentives and culture—through a transformation in ownership, governance, and management—will be required for banks to restore confidence. Although changes in ownership, management, and other areas can be achieved quickly, institutionalizing new systems will take longer.

Settling claims arising from frozen foreign currency accounts. Households have about DM 4 billion in frozen foreign-currency accounts that continue to constitute claims on banks and the government. While the settlement of banks' claims on the former National Bank of Yugoslavia will not be resolved any time soon, in the interim there are ways to settle claims of household depositors from their lost deposits. This settlement will be made from the privatization of enterprises and publicly or socially-owned housing (see Box 3.1).

Building up the deposit base and banks' intermediation capacity. The monetary survey prepared in April 1996 estimated that deposits net of state and Entity governments were DM 325.9 million in the Federation and DM 210.2 million in Republika Srpska. These figures average out to about DM 134 (US$89) per capita—too low for banks to serve as intermediaries. Thus, the magnitude of this problem needs to be recognized, and medium-term targets for developing a viable deposit base need to be established. Doing so will require rapid implementation of the three foundations of banking-sector reform: privatizing existing banks and structures; attracting strategic investment; and developing an enabling environment.

Unifying the payments system. The current payments system, organized outside the banking system, undermines movement toward a viable interbank market to fill overnight liquidity needs. Such fragmentation also limits the deposits placed with banks. Bosnia and Herzegovina should quickly transform this system into a unified system that runs through banking channels. Developing a fully functioning payments system of this sort should be a short-term objective.

Strengthening asset and risk management. In the former Yugoslavia, banks were traditionally passive institutions lending to their borrower shareholders without evaluating market risk. When principal payments fell due they were commonly rolled over, and when interest payments fell due they were frequently capitalized and rolled back into principal. Performance-related loan classification standards were not consistent with market-based principles, and loan loss provisioning was insufficient to cover nonperforming loans. The result was an overstated balance sheet and assets that were of lower quality than was reflected in available financial information. Further, the subordinated role of banks in this relationship meant that there was little follow up on loans. Since the breakup of the former Yugoslavia efforts have been made to address these weaknesses. Banks have become cautious in their lending practices, and credit files reflect efforts to collect interest and principal. Still, these practices are not yet sufficiently developed.

A sustainable commercial banking system will require that banks improve their risk assessment and credit management systems. Assets need to be profitable to provide banks with the resources needed to increase liquidity and capital adequacy. However, assets cannot generate profits unless credit management is strengthened. Over time, bankers must also learn to structure and manage diversified portfolios (loans, securities, properties) under market conditions and to ensure that these assets are matched with liabilities for ongoing safety and soundness. Strong asset and risk management will require better management, sound governance, and increased accountability for monitoring and evaluation.

Clarifying the role of nonbank financial institutions. The strategy for nonbank financial institutions is currently (and understandably) incomplete. In the past few years efforts have been made to create new legislation for insurance and capital markets, reflecting recognition of the potential importance of these sectors. Given the traditional openness of the economy and the importance of foreign trade, the proposed legislation attempts to foster domestic as well as foreign investment. But, the ability of these sectors to function and provide services is dependent on economic recovery. Reviving and developing nonbank financial institutions will require an open environment for capital investment, irrespective of origin. Medium-term objectives should include: finalizing the legal and regulatory framework for private insurance, pension funds, and institutional investors; and building up the institutional infrastructure needed for information disclosure and market analysis. These efforts should also help strengthen the banking sector by reducing the dependence of private enterprises on banks and providing the banks with options to diversify their portfolios.

Part Three

Creating Fiscally Sustainable Social Assistance Programs

Unemployment throughout the country is extremely high with few jobs available for a growing number of demobilized soldiers and refugees. Some employment will be created by the reconstruction program; in addition policy reform should focus on encouraging employment by reducing high taxes on labor, stimulating the development of small businesses, and replacing obsolete labor-market regulations which now discourage employers from hiring. These same measures will also help reduce the extent to which labor moves to the informal sector, thus strengthening tax collections. In the short term, available resources cannot reasonably cover unemployment benefits according to the prewar benefit formula. Direct assistance to the unemployed and their families will have to be targeted and coordinated with social assistance efforts.

The prewar pension system was not financially sustainable because of a rising pensioner-to-worker ratio and relatively high benefits. The collapse of the pay-as-you-go scheme was accelerated by the sudden decline in the number of contributors and their wages after 1991. The three schemes which survive today will not be able to provide an adequate minimum benefit for several years to come. At the same time, the payroll tax rates earmarked to finance pensions cannot be raised, and indeed should be reduced if possible. In the short term, limited resources should be used to ensure minimum pension levels to alleviate poverty among the old and disabled. In order to do this, eligibility on the basis of early retirement or disability must be restricted, the revenue base should be broadened and any revenue growth should be used to increase minimum pensions. This floor of protection could eventually be supplemented by a carefully designed second tier which would serve as a vehicle for retirement savings. Serious consideration should be given to both a Federation-wide pension scheme and a harmonization across the two Entities. This would reduce risks by expanding the pool of insured persons, would reduce administrative costs, and would allow for labor-market mobility. Similar policies aimed at ensuring a minimum level of income, better targeting, and more stringent benefit formulas should be implemented for other social programs, and social welfare institutions should be reformed to reduce cost and increase their operating efficiency. In view of the existence of multiple social assistance programs in the country, a review of all existing programs is currently underway. Reforms may very well be needed to rationalize these assistance programs.

Chapter VIII

Labor-Market Reform

The unemployment rates in Bosnia and Herzegovina today—hovering over near 50 percent—would be unimaginable elsewhere in Europe. Serious measures are needed to expand employment as quickly as possible over the coming months. This expansion should not come at the cost of collecting revenue, however—that is, policies should encourage a flexible labor market and the growth of small private employers as part of the formal economy. Such policies will require adapting employment and labor laws to the demands of a growing market economy.

Major labor-market reforms are needed to address six factors that are likely to inhibit employment growth:

- High marginal taxes on labor;

- Restrictive labor contracts with inflexible or expensive dismissal procedures;

- Arbitrary minimum wages and wage schedules and overly generous vacations, maternity, and other types of leave;

- Restrictions on hiring unemployed workers and on listing job vacancies;

- Insufficient or incompatible education and training; and

- Restrictions on labor-management relations.

Since both Entities are considering new legislation in these areas, both are well-positioned to implement needed reforms.

Labor Market Suffers From the War and Too Many Restrictions

The war had a devastating impact on people, employment, and productivity throughout Bosnia and Herzegovina, and significantly affected the size and composition of the labor force. Although complete demographic data are not available, the Statistical Office in Sarajevo estimates that about 2.25 million people were living in the Federation in the spring of 1996. Another 1 million people are in Republika Srpska. Thus, Bosnia and Herzegovina's population today is about three-quarters of its prewar (1991) level.

Unemployment has soared as formal employment has collapsed

In relative terms, the number of employees working in the formal sector of the economy has declined much more than the population (Table 8.1). The ratio of formal-sector workers to the estimated total labor force, sometimes called the coverage ratio, fell from around 70 percent of the labor force in 1991 to just 36 percent in 1996.[32]   Even this figure might overstate employment, however, given that many workers have not been paid for many months. Formal sector workers form the tax base for payroll taxes and contributions, which account for more than one third of government revenues.   Thus the low coverage ratio implies significant forgone revenue for government-funded programs such as pensions, health care, and education, and to the government budget itself.

Table 8.1 Labor Market Indicators in Bosnia and Herzegovina

	BiH	Bosniac Majority Area	Croat Majority Area	Federation	RS	BiH	BiH
	1991			1996			1996 / 91
In thousands							
Population	4377	1850	400	2250	1000	3250	*74%*
Working Age (20-59)[1]	2404	1016	220	1236	549	1785	*74%*
Labor Force[1]	1882	795	172	967	430	1397	*74%*
Formal Employment[2]	1308	255	52	307	199	506	*39%*
Registered Unemployed[3]	283	141	26	167	n.a.	n.a.	n.a.
Informal or Unemployed[4]	574	540	120	660	231	891	*155%*
In percent							
Unemployment Rate, Narrow[5]	18%	36%	33%	35%	n.a.	n.a.	n.a.
Unemployment Rate, Broad[6]	30%	68%	70%	68%	54%	64%	*209%*
Taxpayers/Labor Force (coverage ratio)	70%	32%	30%	32%	46%	36%	*52%*
In DM							
Average Net Wage[7]	666	206	330	227	30	149	*22%*

Notes:
1/ See text for estimation methodology.
2/ For Bosniac-majority areas, refers to employment in September 1996 excluding Ministry of Defense and Interior; for Croat-majority
areas, refers to total employment in April 1996 including 19,000 soldiers and police; for Republika Srpska refers to total employees in early 1996.
3/ Preliminary figures from Institute of Statistics based on end-October 1996 data.
4/ Labor force minus formal sector employment.
5/ Registered unemployed divided by total estimated labor force.
6/ Informal and unemployed divided by total estimated labor force.
7/ Net wage refers to take home pay after employee contributions. For Bosniac-majority areas, data refer to September 1996, and for Croat-
majority areas and Republika Srpska data refer to April 1996.
Source: Institute of Statistics, Entity Labour Bureaus, World Bank, and IMF staff estimates.

---

[32]   Applying the prewar age distribution to the current total population estimate yields an estimate for the size of the economically active population in the country. However, this is likely to overstate the number of younger people in Bosnia and Herzegovina, especially males, because these individuals are more likely to have migrated or died during the course of the war. Using the labor force participation rates available from a 1990 survey of FYR Macedonia, another demographically young and relatively poor Republic of the former Yugoslavia, suggests an estimated labor force of approximately 1.4 million, of which roughly 1 million would be found in the Federation. In view of the deterioration of health conditions during the war, this estimate is likely to be an upper bound. By contrast, the return of refugees in 1996-97 would tend to increase the size of the labor force.

Unemployment and informal activity grew dramatically as formal employment declined. By mid-1996, the ratio of registered unemployed[33] to a narrowly defined concept of the formal labor force (formal employment plus registered unemployed) had reached about 35 percent in the Federation. This rate will surely rise as unemployment registration continues and demobilization is completed. In the Bosniac-majority areas, about one third of the registered unemployed were demobilized soldiers, with many thousands more to come. According to the broadest definition of unemployment, based on the difference between formal employment and the estimated labor force, two thirds of the labor force is unemployed—as compared with less than one third in 1991 (see Table 8.1). Of course, some people who are not working in formal activities are not, statistically speaking, unemployed. Rather, they are working in the informal labor market.

The collapse of formal-sector employment occurred in all areas of the country. While the Bosniac-majority area appeared to have lost the largest proportion of formal sector jobs, Republika Srpska estimates of employment in the formal sector are probably also inflated in terms of real employment activity by employees who remain on the books, but have not been paid. Employment in the Bosniac-majority area has already begun to recover as transport and communication channels are being restored. Officials in the Croat-majority area expect a 15 percent growth in employment in the second half of 1996, but this does not take into account the demobilization process. Republika Srpska officials also expected significant growth in employment in the second half of 1996. Notwithstanding these developments, there is little disagreement that unemployment will remain an overwhelming problem throughout Bosnia and Herzegovina for the foreseeable future and that military demobilization and refugee repatriation will only exacerbate the situation.

Trends in Wages

For those able to find employment, wages remain generally low, compared to the prewar situation. In the Bosniac-majority areas, however, a low wage base and the positive impact of reconstruction efforts have combined to generate rather rapid increases in the average wage. Average net wages in this area rose from DM 4 in May 1994 to DM 100 in the spring of 1996 and to about DM 200 by September 1996. Figure 8.1 shows that these dramatic improvements restored wage levels close to those prevailing at the beginning 1992, but these gains represent only a small step toward recovering prewar wage levels.

Available data for formal-sector workers in the Croat-majority areas suggest that the average wage there declined less severely than in the Bosniac-majority areas, resulting in considerable regional wage differentials in the Federation by the end of the war. Although earnings in the Croat-majority areas were significantly higher in spring 1996, at an estimated DM 330,[34] the recovery of wages in the Bosniac-majority areas during 1996 reduced the disparity significantly. The ratio of wages in these two areas fell from 6:1 to 3:1 by the middle of 1996 and to 3:2 by the autumn of 1996. The factors driving this convergence, including the

---

[33]   This estimate represents a preliminary figure based on the first attempts in the Federation since 1992 to register the unemployed.

[34]   This figure includes the relatively high wages of military and police which were estimated at DM 450 and DM 370, respectively. To the extent that demobilization occurs and outside financing is curtailed, the average wage in the Croat-majority area will be somewhat lower.

large boost in wages stemming from the relaxation of wartime constraints in the central area of Bosnia, should result in a continuation of this trend. Consequently, wage rates are likely to be similar throughout the Federation in months to come.

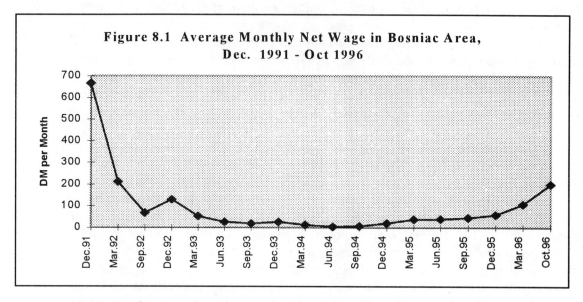

Figure 8.1 Average Monthly Net Wage in Bosniac Area, Dec. 1991 - Oct 1996

Wages in Republika Srpska, however, are unlikely to match those of the Federation in the near future. According to data provided by the Statistical Office in Banja Luka, the average monthly net wage for the first two months of 1996 was about 91 dinar (or approximately DM 25). Although wages appear to have risen during 1996, they are still significantly lower than those in the Federation. Wage recovery in Republika Srpska is likely to depend on the availability of external financing for reconstruction in 1997.

The net wage decline in all areas of Bosnia and Herzegovina is even more striking given the fall in real wages which occurred in the decade immediately preceding the war (Figure 8.2). The average net wage for the entire country was only about one fifth of prewar levels. Despite recent improvements, average wage levels would have to grow by 4-5 percent per month in real terms for the next three years to recover prewar levels and over a much longer period before reaching levels experienced in the late 1970s.

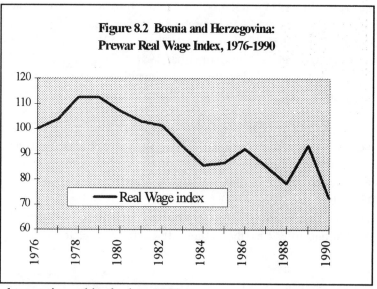

Figure 8.2 Bosnia and Herzegovina: Prewar Real Wage Index, 1976-1990

Real Wage index

The authorities throughout Bosnia and Herzegovina are well aware of the urgent need to reduce unemployment and increase real wages. In recent months, a number of priority measures have been taken, including retraining, public-service employment, and small business development. But much more should and can be done to improve the functioning of labor markets throughout Bosnia and Herzegovina. Measures taken to encourage small businesses and develop flexible labor market would also serve the twin goals of reducing unemployment and stimulating formal labor-market activity. The next section highlights some of the priority areas of reform.

Promoting Employment Generation by Liberalization

The labor market is regulated under a similar legal framework in both Republika Srpska and the Federation, implying that the reform agenda should be broadly similar. To the extent that the current legal framework is operative, it remains, to a great extent, a carry over from the labor-market legislation used in the former Yugoslavia. Both Entities are aware that current laws do not meet the needs of a market economy and are in the process of reformulating their labor codes. The objective is to promote a flexible labor market conducive to full employment and economic growth. The Federation faces the additional challenge of reconciling differences between two parallel institutional structures.

Payroll taxes must be lowered to reasonable levels

The adverse impact of high payroll taxes on employment and economic activity has been discussed at length in Chapter III on fiscal management. The principle message of that discussion is that payroll taxes that effectively double the cost of labor are untenable. They artificially drive up the cost of labor, thereby depressing demand and, at the same time they increase the incidence of tax evasion, thus reducing the tax base further. When these taxes are used for expenditures not commonly funded through contributions, they should be largely replaced with other sources of revenue such as increased taxes on consumption (general sales taxes or excises). Expenditures for pensions, unemployment, and health insurance, which are commonly funded through payroll-tax contributions, should be gradually reduced to affordable levels over a five-year phase-in period as the economy expands.

Wages and benefits should be freely set

Under current laws in both Entities, minimum wages are set administratively each month. However, market-determined wages are making headway in the private sector. Official wage scales should be eliminated as soon as possible to ease the concern of private employers and to remove a needless restriction on managers of public enterprises. Private employers are likely to set market-based wages regardless of whether such wage-setting practices are legally sanctioned.

While there has been considerable debate among economists in recent years on the impact of the minimum wage on employment, most agree that a higher minimum wage (relative to the market-determined wage for low-skilled workers) has a negative impact on employment generation. If a minimum wage is meant to signal that some salaries are not acceptable to society, it should not be subject to frequent changes nor set arbitrarily. Moreover, the minimum wage should affect only a small percentage of the work force. If the minimum wage is too high, unemployment will rise, illegal and gray market activity will flourish, and more people will be stuck in subsistence occupations, such as farming, at arguably lower income levels.

The liberal leave provisions mandated by the current labor code or as part of social legislation also restrict employment growth. For example, vacation leave in Republika Srpska is a minimum of 14 working days (in addition to other leave time and holidays) and in the Federation a minimum of 18 working days. In both Entities, vacation time increases to 30 days maximum (in addition to many other circumstances that entitle workers to additional paid leave). Sick leave and maternity leave are also generous, and potentially costly for small employers that must train new workers to fill vacancies. Maternity leave lasts one year (more in some cases) and requires that the employee be rehired at the same job at the end of the period. Sick leave is paid by employers; maternity leave is, in theory, paid for by the health-insurance fund. Although employers do not face salary costs for workers on maternity leave, maternity leave provisions indirectly increase employers' payroll tax obligations because the health-insurance fund is financed by payroll taxes. Further, hiring replacement workers is costly. Maternity leave provisions will likely cause employers to avoid hiring female workers.

These restrictive leave and benefit requirements make it difficult for small employers to maintain a work force, substitute for workers on extended vacations, and pay for sick leave. Moreover, such liberal leave policies are inappropriate in an economy with high unemployment and low incomes. Both Entities should be careful not to set their standards too high, but rather should target their legislation to meet the needs of emerging private enterprises.

Unemployment compensation should be coordinated with other social assistance programs

It would be impossible to estimate how many workers would have been eligible for unemployment benefits during the war. In any event, few if any payments were actually made. Even today, few people are receiving unemployment compensation as the government authorities try to reconstruct the necessary databases. Eligibility criteria for unemployment insurance are fairly stringent, with only employees dismissed because of restructuring eligible for cash assistance. Still, the unemployment benefit formula provides for sizable benefits that would distort labor market behavior even if they were affordable. In the short term, even minimum benefits are not affordable given the massive unemployment in both Entities. At current tax rates, the revenues earmarked for unemployment benefits would cover less than 10 percent of the registered unemployed even if only a minimum cash benefit were provided. Moreover, neither the financing nor the institutional apparatus exists to handle the unemployment problem. Thus, transfers to the unemployed should be coordinated with other social assistance programs.

In the medium term, current legal provisions should be revisited with an eye toward establishing a sustainable system. Further, Employment Bureau budgets should be based on realistic estimates of the cost of benefits and other services. If revenues cannot meet costs, legislative changes should be implemented to lower costs.

Job search mechanisms need to be opened to competition

As in the former Yugoslavia, the Employment Bureau is the only source of job listings for unemployed workers in Bosnia and Herzegovina. Other methods of job search, at least for unemployed workers, are precluded if employers and unemployed workers bypass the Employment Bureau's services. In other words, unemployed workers cannot apply for or accept a job, at least legally, by word of mouth, through the newspaper, or through a private employment service. All three official labor bureaus are designed to operate as monopolies.

In OECD countries--even those with effective government-operated labor exchanges--private employment services account for a substantial portion of job placements. In fact, informal job searches and private services generally account for most job placements. Even in Sweden, the OECD country with the most monopolistic job search policies, more than one third of placements are made outside the State labor exchange. If employment is to recover quickly in Bosnia and Herzegovina, the development of a variety of job placement avenues needs to be supported by legislation that encourages the proliferation of information and placements. Current legislation prohibiting private job placement agencies should be replaced by regulatory standards to prevent fraud and abuse.

The need for private job placement services does not imply that the operations of the government-run labor exchanges should be downgraded. Rather, the government system should develop efficient job listings and worker assistance mechanisms. Funding for this function should be a high priority. The two Employment Bureaus in the Federation (one in Sarajevo and one in Mostar) should be linked immediately, and may be united in the near future, to provide services for job seekers throughout the Federation.

Training and education should be upgraded and expanded

Labor market expansion should be supported by a work force that has the necessary skills and education to meet the demands of a flexible market economy. The three Employment Bureaus are starting to refocus their activities on developing active labor-market programs. Refugees and former employees of socially-owned enterprises are in particular need of retraining. Programs must be developed with caution, however, to ensure that they are demand driven and cost effective. In many transition economies, education and training have been too narrowly focused and do not target the skills demanded by employers. Further, adult education and retraining cannot be the sole responsibility of the Employment Bureaus. New facilities focusing on adult education need to be developed regionally, preferably by the private sector.

In the future, the labor force must be replenished with well-educated graduates from the Entity education systems. These systems are in need of both immediate reconstruction and long-term systemic restructuring. About 70 percent of education facilities have suffered damage. Population movements have interrupted instruction in primary and secondary schools, and the trauma of war has hindered pupils' learning. In addition, teachers' salaries are low and often have not been paid. Finally, many trained teachers have left the country. These issues are being addressed on an emergency basis with reconstruction assistance and donated teachers' time.

In the longer term, however, reformed curriculums and better teacher training will be needed to hone the skills required for a market economy. Government officials are beginning to recognize these needs, but further exposure to education reforms and innovations throughout Central and Eastern Europe and elsewhere would be helpful. For example, education officials in Republika Srpska are concerned about their ability to provide English-language classes and computer training. But these are not the only elements needed to produce an active labor force with the skills to enter a market economy. Consequently, broader systemic reforms must be developed.

Labor-management relations must become more flexible

A single labor contract among unions, employers, and government (rather than industrywide or companywide contracts) has traditionally been part of the regulatory framework in Bosnia and Herzegovina. A new collective contract of this type is being implemented in Republika Srpska, however, and in the future a collective contract may be used in the Federation. If the collective agreement includes provisions that inhibit the expansion of employment or foster informal market activity, those provisions should be changed, and only minimum, across-the-board standards should be used for all employers. While the right to organize is a fundamental right of labor, uniform conditions may no longer be appropriate for all employees. Industrial or occupational unions can collectively bargain for wages and employment conditions above the minimums established for their sector. Thus, restrictive collective contracts can be counterproductive in a market economy, particularly for an economy that is trying to emerge from wartime destruction.

Unionization varies significantly among OECD countries, from low rates in France (9.8 percent) and the United States (15.6 percent) to high rates in Sweden (82.5 percent). Many other OECD countries have unionization rates between 35 and 45 percent of the labor force. In some countries, collective bargaining takes place primarily at the plant or enterprise level, while in others it is on a sectorwide basis. Industrywide bargaining is more prevalent in European countries with high unemployment. High unionization and industrywide collective bargaining are likely to reduce competition in the product market and can stifle job creation in labor-intensive activities.[35] New Zealand's experience demonstrates how rapid changes in the bargaining structure can occur as a country shifts from multiemployer contracts to single employer bargaining. The role of labor unions in Bosnia and Herzegovina should be considered carefully, with a need to balance the use of unions (to provide workers with bargaining power in the face of monopsonistic employers) with the need to avoid excessively powerful unions (which limit labor market flexibility).

---

[35] Source: OECD, 1994, *The OECD Jobs Study; Part II: The Adjustment Potential of the Labor Market*, Chapter 6, Paris.

Chapter IX

Social Protection Programs

A number of government programs provide cash benefits and social services in both the Federation and Republika Srpska. The most important of these are the vestiges of the prewar social insurance system, which included pension, health care, and unemployment programs. In 1996, the revenues earmarked for these programs accounted for more than one quarter of all revenues and about 8 percent of estimated GDP. In addition, new programs have been established to deal with the poverty, homelessness, and war-related disabilities that are the legacies of war. For many people, these benefits are the most important form of relief from extreme poverty. Until the economy recovers, however, the programs that make up the social safety net will meet only a fraction of the vast demand for social services.

Given these constraints, social policy over the next few years will have to focus on the most urgent social priorities. The social safety net must protect the most vulnerable members of society in the immediate postwar period. In the medium term, a stronger financial situation will allow for a greater scope of activity--but not a return to the extensive social welfare system that prevailed in the former Yugoslavia, a system that would have been unsustainable even if the war never occurred. The shifting role of the State in the social sphere has been difficult to manage in all the transition economies, and will likely be especially complicated in Bosnia and Herzegovina. However, the extent to which the old system has been destroyed might provide a unique opportunity for fundamental reform.

Building a basic safety net to weather the next few years could be the first step in the reform process. A coherent set of programs designed to fill basic needs could serve as the foundation of the new system. Supplementary benefits and programs could be introduced later, as the economy recovers. The institutional and financial underpinnings of these new programs should be considered carefully before legislation is implemented, however. Fiscally responsible programs can be designed as the economy and population stabilize and better data become available.

The Social Safety Net Must Be Restructured

By prewar standards most of Bosnia and Herzegovina's population now lives in poverty. Because of resource constraints, short-term social policy must focus on protecting the most vulnerable groups and maximizing the impact of available resources. The following steps should be taken immediately:

• Using available resources to increase the minimum pension and make it consistent within Entities;

• Restricting eligibility for new pensions by curtailing early retirement (including the purchase of service-year credits) and enforcing strict disability standards;

• Moving the budget of the pension fund in the Bosniac-majority areas off-budget;

- Prioritizing the services to be provided through the health system and establishing an affordable minimum basket of services to be provided in each Entity;

- Taking advantage of economies of scale in service provision whenever possible;

- Coordinating information and policies for social assistance and social insurance programs; and

- Using the Federation's recent experience with the Emergency Social Fund and studies on poverty to create an effective and well-targeted social assistance program.

In addition, certain policy measures could be announced immediately but phased in over time. These include:

- Introducing legislation outlining the social insurance institutions in each Entity and their relationship to each other and to Entity and canton government institutions (including budgetary relations);

- Gradually increasing the retirement age to 62 for both men and women over the next five years;

- Designing and eventually introducing health and pension programs to supplement the first-tier minimum benefits that are the focus of short-term policy;

- Introducing legislation allowing and regulating voluntary membership in private health and pension plans and creating a corresponding government regulating body; and

- Improving collection and enforcement of payroll taxes, especially for the emerging private sector.

Implementation of these policies will vary according to the economic and institutional conditions in each Entity. Medium-term planning will require decisions about the appropriate administrative structure for unemployment, health care, and pension institutions, particularly in the Federation. (The Federation's social insurance system has splintered into two separate subsystems outside any clear legal framework.) Finally, the question of arrears (such as unpaid pensions) should be tackled separately and in the framework of settling of other claims on the government (Box 3.1).

Old Age, Disability, and Survivor Pensions Are Unsustainable

The three pension schemes that existed at the end of 1996 were remnants of the pay-as-you-go scheme that operated in Bosnia and Herzegovina before the war. This scheme, like many in the region, was already experiencing financial strain by 1991--mainly because of a dramatic increase in the number of pensioners per employed person (Figure 9.1). The sharp increase in 1990-91 suggests that early retirement patterns during the initial stages of economic restructuring were exacerbating this trend, which has since occurred in other transition economies. Even without the war, the tax system would have had trouble dealing with the new structure of the economy, especially small firms in the private sector. The likely result would have been an erosion of the tax base, leading to higher payroll tax rates or bigger deficits. Similarly, the

the average pension to the average wage), low retirement ages, and a declining number of contributors. Governments in Croatia and FYR Macedonia have experienced this dilemma and have implemented restrictive measures to ensure solvency.

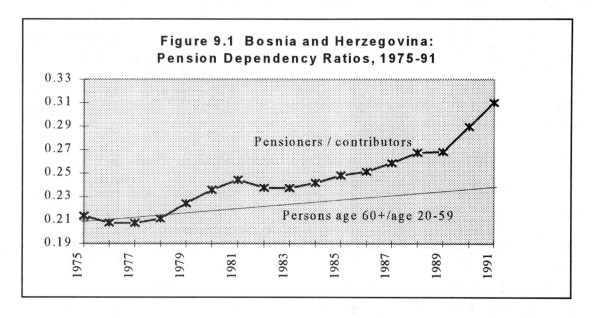

Low contributions, employment, and wages have weakened the system. The financial status of a pay-as-you-go pension scheme depends on the growth of the covered wage bill--that is, the number of contributing workers multiplied by the average wage subject to payroll taxes. Both the number of contributing workers and the average wage collapsed during the war, severely reducing the value of the average pension paid to hundreds of thousands of pensioners (Table 9.1). After the war, the number of formal sector employees was a scant 39 percent of prewar levels, while the number of pensioners remained nearly constant. As a result, the system dependency ratio more than doubled between 1991 and 1996.

Table 9.1 Key Pension System Indicators

	BiH	Federation	RS	BiH	BiH
	1991	1996			1996 / 91
Population (thousands)	4377	2250	1000	3250	74%
Number of Pensioners (thousands)[1]	408	246	153	399	98%
Number of Formal Employees (thousands) [2]	1308	307	199	506	39%
System Dependency (percentage)[3]	31%	80%	77%	79%	253%
Average Pension (DM)[4]	473	90	33	68	14%

1/ Federation pensioners estimated at 195,000 and 51,000 from Bosniac- and Croat-majority areas respectively.

2/ See notes in Table 8.1. Formally employed persons may not correspond to active contributor population.

3/ Ratio of pensioners to formally employed persons who are used here as a proxy for contributors.

4/ Federation figure based on estimates for September 1996. The Republika Srpska figure based on November 1996 payment.

Source: Institute of Statistics, Pension Bureaus, World Bank, and IMF staff estimates.

Significant lags have delayed payments in each pension scheme (old age, disability, survivor) and some pensioners were completely cut off during the war.[36] Pensions paid since 1992 have been extremely low and undoubtedly below any reasonable poverty line.[37] Further, the real value of real pensions declined significantly during the war.

Solvency rests on stringency. The relationship between the pension fund and government budgets in the two Entities is not well defined. The schemes operating in Republika Srpska and in the Croat-majority areas of the Federation are off-budget and collect their own revenues. Such arrangements might lead to greater fiscal responsibility. The scheme operating in the Bosniac-majority areas has been integrated with all other tax revenues, and pension funds are allocated from these revenues in an ad hoc manner.

The resource constraints faced by all three schemes are likely to continue over the next few years (Table 9.2). Despite the recent expansion in employment in the Federation, the ratio of pensioners to employed workers is about 85 percent across Bosnia and Herzegovina. Given the depressed levels of average wages and already high tax rates, this ratio means that average pensions will remain quite low in the near future, assuming that financing is on a pay-as-you-go basis. In order for the average pension to increase substantially, either the system-dependency ratio must fall or real wages must increase. Although wage growth depends on increased productivity, the system-dependency ratio can be improved if the number of formal-sector workers grows and is not offset by excessive growth in the number of pensioners.

Table 9.2 Indicators of Pension System Finances: January to September 1996

	Bosniac-Majority Areas	Croat-Majority Areas	Federation	RS	BiH
	January - September 1996				
1. Number of Pensioners [1/]	193,000	51,000	244,000	153,000	397,000
2. Number of Contributors [1/]	239,000	51,000	290,000	175,000	465,000
3. System Dependency (1) (2)	81%	100%	84%	87%	85%
4. Average Net Pension [2/]	41	73	48	15	35
5. Average Covered Wage [2/ 3/]	159	512	221	69	164
6. Replacement Rate [4/]	26%	14%	22%	22%	21%
7. Contribution Rate [5/]	24.5%	16.7%	21%	22%	22%
8. Covereged Wage Bill/GDP [6/]	22%	19%	21%	10%	18%
9. Pension Payments/GDP	4.7%	2.7%	3.8%	1.9%	3.3%

1/ Estimated.
2/ Average estimated for first nine months in monthly DM; pensions after transfer to health fund.
3/ Covered wage bill in DM divided by estimated number of workers.
4/ Average net pension in DM divided by average covered wage.
5/ Contribution rate for military in Croat-majority areas appears to be 15.3 percent vs 17.5 percent for other workers.
6/ Covered wage bill is social security contributions divided by wage tax rate.
Source: Institute of Statistics, Pension Bureaus, World Bank, and IMF staff estimates.

[36]   Pension payments, including lump-sum payments for past periods, are now being made in areas that were inaccessible during the war (such as Bihać and Gorazde).

[37]   The Central Statistical Office in Sarajevo currently estimates a "basket of essential products." To date, however, no statistics have been developed for Bosnia and Herzegovina based on internationally accepted consumption-based or poverty-line measures.

Contribution rates are excessive. The payroll tax for pensions is one of several taxes levied on labor that together account for about 100 percent of average net wages. Because high payroll taxes encourage tax evasion and discourage employment, they should be cut considerably. As the economy recovers, some of the improvement in the financial health of the pension fund should translate into lower tax rates (rather than higher benefits). Reducing marginal tax rates on labor, along with the measures outlined in Chapter VIII, should generate employment in the formal sector and broaden the tax base for medium-term financing of social benefits. Exemptions and other factors that narrow the tax base should be avoided.

Ensuring Minimum Pension and Better Targeting are Short-Term Priorities for Pension Reform

Pensions will continue to face financial difficulties over the next few years. Short-term policies must incorporate compromises that recognize the constraints on the revenue side while providing a floor of protection. The medium term might allow for higher benefits, subject to the need to reduce payroll tax rates and encourage formal employment.

Minimum protection is essential. In the short term, each Entity should implement a minimum pension that provides a floor of income protection. Any increase in revenues due to wage or employment growth should be used to support that minimum pension and reduce fund dependency on budgetary resources and donor support. Second-tier earnings-based pensions should be paid only after this minimum-pension obligation is met. The plan in Croat-majority areas pays a flat-rate benefit. In Republika Srpska and Sarajevo, pension payments are tied to earnings. If funding is not sufficient to pay both the minimum pension and the earnings-related benefits, benefits should be eliminated or sharply curtailed. If funding is sufficient to pay for both tiers of benefits, the minimum pension should be indexed more generously than the second-tier.[38]

The minimum pension could be set for the entire country or for each Entity. It should ideally be related to an internationally accepted poverty line based on a basket of minimal consumption. A reasonable goal for an average replacement rate for old-age benefits would be 40 to 50 percent of the average wage. The minimum pension might be targeted at 25 to 30 percent of the average wage. In the short term, the Federation could set its target at the current flat rate in the Croat-majority areas. The weak finances of Republika Srpska, however, cannot support a minimum pension at this level and will be challenged to offer even lower benefits.

Other measures are needed to achieve short-term financial balance. The pension funds in each Entity must improve their contribution compliance procedures and restrict pension eligibility if they are to pay for even a first tier of benefits. Methods to improve compliance should be coordinated with changes in tax administration throughout the country. Compliance will be particularly difficult to enforce in the growing private sector. These new audit and enforcement procedures will have to be developed and implemented.

---

[38] Several countries (Estonia, Mexico) that have faced dramatic declines in the real value of their average pensions have implemented differential indexing pensions. Other countries (Hungary) have chosen to restrict benefit increases for pensioners at the top of the distribution. Differences in indexing develop from the principle that low-income groups must be protected more than those with higher lifetime earnings.

Several changes in eligibility requirements are needed: disability criteria must be tightened; early retirement must be curtailed or eliminated; and the normal retirement age must be increased. These measures are required to create an affordable system and to ensure that benefits are provided only to people who can no longer work productively. While countries are often tempted to substitute pensions for unemployment benefits--thereby disguising unemployment and providing a more socially acceptable solution--the pension system should not be used to protect the unemployed. This is particularly important for the pension funds in Bosnia and Herzegovina since a funding gap might still exist, even after the proposed measures to improve revenues and restrict benefits are introduced.

Additional tiers should eventually be introduced. In the medium term, improving finances should allow the Entities to supplement their first-tier pension with a program designed to provide retirement income related to past contributions. This second tier could take many forms, but its size should take into account the need to lower payroll taxes. Once the foundations of a sound financial sector are in place, a privately managed and funded scheme could be considered. The design and implementation of a new pension system will require much preparation. Basic demographic and economic data will need to be collected and analyzed in order to provide actuarial projections that can guide policymakers toward a fiscally sustainable pension system. The Federation government has already established a Pension Reform Working Group for this purpose. Whatever mechanisms are used, they will have to be revised as the dynamics of the economy unfold.

First- and second-tier pensions could be administered at the Entity level. Participants in both of the pension funds operating in the Federation would benefit from higher pensions with common collection and benefit payment arrangements. Public and private pension schemes around the world show that such economies of scale in administration exist and lead to lower administrative costs.

Planning for a funded tier could begin as financial markets and institutions start to develop. This would involve introducing legislation allowing and regulating the activities of private pension providers and other types of long-term savings instruments. It would also entail assigning supervisory responsibilities to government agencies and building the necessary capacity to perform these functions.

Separate pension systems should be consolidated. Administering the pension system at a higher level of government would provide additional benefits for participants in the existing schemes, as well as for the economy as a whole. If an economywide system were in place, workers would incur lower costs in transferring rights to a pension from one area to another. Moreover, labor mobility is impeded when multiple systems operate in parallel. Finally, the small number of participants, especially in the Croat-majority areas, might encourage volatility given the limited ability to pool risk with such a small number of participants.

The establishment of the Federation Pension Agency might provide the foundation for harmonizing or integrating the two schemes in the Federation. In the meantime, however, the Sarajevo-based fund should be moved off-budget and earmarked revenues should be automatically deposited in its account in the payments system. This move would clarify fiscal responsibilities and facilitate coordination between the two funds in working out mechanisms for determining eligibility and membership according to cantonal residence or other criteria.[39]

Sustainable Health-Care Financing Requires a New Approach

In 1991, health expenditures in Bosnia and Herzegovina totaled 6.5 percent of GDP, or US$150 per capita--rather high for Central Europe. In addition to the costs associated with extensive infrastructure, these high costs developed from norms dictating the number of beds, items of equipment, and size and staff in health-care institutions, all of which combined to create perverse incentives. Overspecialization and excessive utilization, referrals, and prescriptions also contributed to high costs. As part of the wider Yugoslav system, a health-insurance system operated through a parastatal fund that had limited autonomy. Funds for health care were raised through a compulsory payroll-based scheme, with contributions from employers and workers passed through the health-insurance fund in Sarajevo. With minuscule official unemployment, 74 percent of health-insurance income came from State enterprises, 19 percent from the pension fund, and 7 percent from agriculture and the private sector. A plan to deal with the increasing imbalance between health costs and revenues was initiated shortly before the war. It called for strengthening the role of the health-insurance fund as a procurement mechanism, encouraging private provision of health services, ensuring that the expenditure of the insurance fund did not exceed its income, and increasing fees and individual payments. Implementation of this plan was prevented by the war.

The unified system collapsed during the war. Shortly after, three systems emerged--two in the Federation and one in Republika Srpska. In the Federation's primarily Bosniac-majority areas, the insurance fund was merged with the Ministry of Health in January 1994. In the Croat-majority areas, a separate insurance fund has been in operation since 1993.

A system in crisis

The health-care systems in both Entities are experiencing severe financial crisis. Throughout Bosnia and Herzegovina, but especially in Republika Srpska, emergency relief and humanitarian aid still cover most health-care costs. This situation cannot and will not continue indefinitely. While during the war physicians provided their services largely without pay, neither Entity can rely on such services over the longer term. In March 1996, physicians' salaries in the Federation increased to about DM 520 per month, but this trend has not been matched in other areas. Overall, the maintenance of emergency aid and the re-establishment of normalcy in the payment of salaries has been of primary concern.

Minimal levels of self-funding have been maintained through high payroll tax rates in both Entities. Republika Srpska's health-insurance fund is managed on a regional basis and has been used primarily to pay staff salaries. Fund expenditures have paid for about 20 percent of health-care costs; emergency aid has covered the rest. In addition, serious medical cases have been sent to the Federal Republic of Yugoslavia for care when facilities in Republika Srpska were insufficient. Own expenses are expected to rise, however, since Belgrade is no longer willing to pay for such care. In the Croat-majority areas of the Federation, a health-insurance

---

[39] Important questions would remain, however, on the governance of the off-budget schemes, and a temporary legal solution would have to be worked out.

fund was established during the war, primarily to pay staff salaries. In the Bosniac-majority areas, the health-insurance fund was incorporated in the government budget. In both parts of the Federation, as in Republika Srpska, most medical care continues to be provided through donor assistance.

Each Entity must develop a strategy to phase out their reliance on external aid, determine future financing arrangements, and fund a health-insurance system that provides a basic care package at an affordable cost. These strategies will be constrained by limited resources and the need to lower payroll taxes. Thus, the funding base for health care must be broadened as soon as possible. Options include using general budget revenues to cover some of the medical benefits of the nonemployed, charging user fees and other forms of cost sharing, and introducing supplementary insurance plans would not be subsidized.

Achieving sustainable financing will require major adjustments

Federation. The Federation's main problem is having two health-care funds. While it is true that basic health care should be provided at the canton level, revenues might not cover expenditures in every canton at all times. In fact, some cantons might never be able to raise sufficient revenue to pay for basic care. Further, the large interregional disparities in health-care provision mean that decentralizing the provision of minimum health services would threaten key aspects of the social safety net. It could also create unacceptable disparities in service provision within the Federation. As a result, redistributive transfers are needed to provide cross-canton subsidies. A working group has been formed to recommend policy reforms focused on the canton level, but a program has not yet been agreed on.

In the medium to long term, the Federation government plans to introduce a three-tiered system of health insurance. The first tier will ensure that all people have access to a basic package of basic services that is uniform across the Federation. Each canton will also adopt a second tier that will provide coverage for a canton-specified supplementary package of health care, financed by mandatory payroll taxes. A third tier of voluntary private insurance, financed by private premiums, will cover enhanced care and services not included under the compulsory tiers. Compulsory insurance will be managed and administered at the canton level within Federation guidelines. Uniform data-reporting requirements for service utilization, health revenue and expenditure patterns, and standard indicators of health-sector inputs, outcomes, and management will apply to all cantons.

The first tier will be funded by a Federation Health Fund, to be financed by payroll taxes and matching transfers from the budget (up to a limited amount per month). These funds will be divided on a per-capita basis and returned to the cantons to finance basic health services. The Federation government will ensure that any new health-insurance legislation provides for the continued operation of this fund.

Republika Srpska. Republika Srpska's health-insurance system must strike a balance between pressing health-care needs and limited financial resources. The Republika Srpska Ministry of Health plans to oversee one compulsory insurance system and several optional private insurance systems. The compulsory system will cover the entire population, with an administrative structure consisting of one public health fund and eight branch offices. All resources will pass through the central fund. The branch offices will pay, among other things, maternity clinics, travel costs for referred patients, and mobility aids (such as eyeglasses and orthopedic devices) for children. Prices will be set by the central fund. Contributions will be paid by workers and employers, for workers and their families, in the amount of 28 percent of salaries, with equal shares paid by employers and workers. Self-employed people and farmers will also pay contributions. The Republika Srpska government will pay for low income (undefined) people, invalids, and indigent families of soldiers killed during the war, and other groups.

Social Assistance Programs Should be Reexamined and Restructured

As noted, poor people throughout Bosnia and Herzegovina have enormous needs. Not only do the authorities deal with the "normal" poverty needs common to all countries, they also must confront the crushing unemployment, dislocation, and disability caused by the war. Problems will likely get worse in the short run as refugees return to their homes and soldiers continue to be demobilized. Neither Entity has the resources to finance a program of cash transfers to the poor. And, the emergency relief, especially donations of food, that sustained most of the population in recent years is expected to be cut off in the near future.

The network of social welfare offices in the Federation continued to operate during the war, providing services to the extent possible. As with other social service providers (doctors, teachers), social welfare staff worked without salaries during the war. The government maintained institutions for orphans and for people with mental disabilities, but funds were not sufficient to cover all the operating costs of these facilities. Funding is also needed to reconstruct many of these facilities.

The Federation Ministry of Social Affairs is revising social welfare legislation, with initial policies developed by a working group representing interests from throughout the Federation. Future social-welfare programs in the Federation will remain uncertain, however, until revenues can be secured for these purposes. Many of the social programs in place before the war (such as supplies for newborns) are under review, as are alternative programs (such as the substitution of foster care for orphanages). Traditional assistance efforts were targeted at specific groups, including orphans, single parent families, children with disabilities, mentally-disabled adults, and families with development problems. The provision and expansion of social services through volunteer efforts would be a useful supplement to government activities. A cash assistance program was in place before the war but had few users. The Federation recently introduced an emergency assistance program--funded by donors and the World Bank--to disburse payments to poor families through the Emergency Social Fund, providing DM 10 per person to families who meet the income criteria established for the program. This fund is the Federation's only vehicle for cash assistance.

In Republika Srpska, social welfare offices are organized by the municipalities. Republika Srpska recently implemented two new programs providing cash benefits for poor families and assistance for families with infants and children. These programs are similar to those being considered in the Federation. The cash assistance program is funded through a 2 percent payroll tax and other small taxes (for example, on gifts of property). An estimated 330,000 families--25 percent of the population--could be eligible for assistance. A funding gap of 24 million Yugoslav dinars is anticipated based on current calculations. Republika Srpska authorities hope to close this gap though donor financing similar to that provided to the Emergency Social Fund.

The infants and children program is financed by a 3 percent payroll tax. Besides the burden this tax imposes on labor costs, this program needs to be prioritized in light of current resources and needs. This program funds allowances for pregnant women, supplies for newborns, allowances and kindergartens for third and fourth children, and kindergartens for orphans and disabled children. Municipal funding for kindergartens, school excursions, and preventive health care is also required under the new law.

The sustainability of Republika Srpska's new programs has yet to be assessed. The funding of these programs with payroll taxes should be reconsidered, however. Although the tax burden on wages has fallen from 120 percent of net wages to 98 percent through recent legislative changes, this level of payroll taxation is still excessive, particularly in an economy struggling for recovery.

A general review of social welfare programs should be undertaken in both Entities to determine whether funds are well utilized and whether proposed or enacted social programs are affordable and adequately targeted to the poor. This review should also find ways to coordinate different cash transfer programs such as pensions, unemployment benefits, and social assistance. In the short term, cash assistance will have to be funded by donors to provide a floor of protection. In the medium term, these programs must be the responsibility of each Entity. To help evaluate welfare expenditures and develop a plan for the future, a poverty assessment (including analysis of longitudinal surveys of the population) should be performed soon. Further, the Federation must decide whether programs currently funded through the Federation budget, including orphanages and nursing homes, should be transferred to the cantons. If all programs are expected to be canton-based, the only role for the Federation Ministry of Health would be in setting standards.

Part Four

Rebuilding Essential Physical Infrastructure

During the war, transportation, power, and communications infrastructure suffered significant damage. Private resources, possibly through the use of concessions, will be needed to rehabilitate these sectors. Even if the government retains control over some sectors, however, severe resource constraints will prohibit fast progress without sector reforms. Three reforms are essential. First, rates must reflect costs, although some poor users can be subsidized. Second, to ensure the greatest operating efficiency, better inter-Entity coordination is needed to maximize the usefulness of power, communications, and transport networks that cross Entity boundaries. Finally, accounting and management standards in sector enterprises must improve dramatically.

Chapter X

Power, Transport, and Telecommunications

In the 1980's, public utilities in Bosnia and Herzegovina were publicly owned and operated monopolies. Local networks (water and sanitation, district heating, urban transport) were run by municipally owned companies, and national networks (electric power, railways, telecommunications) were run by socially-owned republican companies. Central offices based in Belgrade ensured coordination among the Yugoslav republics. The republican companies lent services to each other, settling balances at the end of each year. Self-management led to overstaffing, overly generous compensation, and inefficiency. Tariffs were often low, and most companies were propped up with government subsidies. Service delivery, however, was generally adequate by regional standards.

When the war broke out, the republican utility companies were divided into separate enterprises, two in the Federation (one in the Bosniac-majority areas and one in the Croat-majority areas) and one in Republika Srpska. The newly established companies (in the Croat-majority areas and in Republika Srpska) took over the assets located in their areas but did not assume their share of liabilities. The war caused substantial damage to infrastructure, particularly along the lines of confrontation and in areas where heavy fighting occurred. As a result, many parts of the country have unreliable power supplies, railways run irregularly between certain parts of the country, and intra-Entity telephone calls are difficult and inter-Entity calls impossible.

Infrastructure Sectors Share Several Weaknesses

Reforms are needed in most or all infrastructure sectors to improve the quality and availability of service, increase efficiency and lower costs, and ensure the financial viability of utilities and other infrastructure enterprises. Essential reforms include increasing revenues, developing better accounting systems, improving inter-Entity cooperation, addressing prewar assets and liabilities, and adjusting management and ownership of utilities.

To fulfill this agenda, the role of governments must be diminished and redefined, political interference must be avoided, and managers must be allowed to follow sound business practices. A substantial amount of work will be required to change current management practices, address overstaffing issues, and design specific programs to make up for the departure of qualified staff during the war.

Increasing revenues through better billing and more realistic pricing

Low billing and collection rates and low tariffs have hurt revenues in many sectors. Moreover, billing and collection rates fell significantly during the war. Household tariffs are often lower than tariffs for other users even though the cost of delivering services is higher. Although many households would be unable to pay for the full cost of basic utilities, waiting until the economy recovers to deal with this issue will only entrench inefficient use. Billing and collection should be increased, and low-income users should be provided with appropriate support (Box 10.1).

Box 10.1 Increasing Revenues in Utility Sectors

To ensure financial viability of the utility sector, revenues will have to be increased. As a first step, the authorities and managers of the company should establish an acceptable timetable to do so. Detailed target deadlines should be set for improving billing and collection rates, eliminating subsidies, and increasing tariff levels. This will improve internal efficiency and reduce the burden on public finances. A modest agenda would be to: (i) cover all cash operating costs by 1998; (ii) make cash flow positive by 1999; and (iii) fully recover costs in the following five-year period--traditionally, this would include operating costs, debt service and around 35 to 40 percent of investment costs.

The tariff policy and regulatory framework should simultaneously achieve several goals:

Tariff distortions should be reduced immediately;

Adequate measures (e.g., lifeline tariffs) should be used to protect low-income consumers; and

Payment of utility bills with vouchers provided to the demobilized soldiers should be strictly avoided, both to avoid inflationary pressure and to ensure that utility companies will be able to cover their operating costs.

Strengthening accounting systems to improve efficiency and regulation

Proper and transparent accounting is essential in all companies. Regulating infrastructure sectors efficiently will require detailed knowledge of companies' finances, including in-depth analysis of outstanding debts, payables, and receivables. Financial data should include these categories. Liabilities to prewar and current employees also need to be specified.

Improving inter-Entity cooperation and coordination

Although the infrastructure systems in each region might be able to operate efficiently as separate companies, this would require substantial cooperation (Box 10.2). Immediate benefits could come from inter-Entity arrangements relinking infrastructure networks. Agreements should be formalized through commercial contracts, with mutually agreed metering and regular payments. Reaching such agreements in the shortest period of time—and thereby ensuring delivery of services—should be the main priority for the utilities. Inter-Entity cooperation, although not necessary for the daily operation of some networks,[40] might be desirable to address policy issues; thus specific sectoral arrangements should be designed whenever needed.[41]

---

[40] Natural gas is an important exception. Although gas is used mainly in the Federation (particularly in Sarajevo), the transmission pipeline is partly located in Republika Srpska. A specific agreement, including provisions on operating procedures to be followed by the two companies (Sarajevogas and Sarajevogas Republika Srpska) and transmission fees should be worked out as soon as possible.

[41] As an example, water and sanitation are managed at the local level by municipally owned water and sanitation enterprises. Before the war, each republic had, in addition to these companies, a water resources institute to address water disputes among and within the republics. Currently, there are two water resource institutes in Bosnia and Herzegovina, one in Republika Srpska and one in the Federation. Inter-Entity cooperation could, therefore, be ensured according to the prewar model.

Box 10.2 The Commission on Public Corporations

Many of the topics contained in this section are being examined by the Commission on Public Corporations set up in accordance with Annex 9 of the Dayton Agreement by the Federation and the Republika Srpska. This Commission consists of five members: two representatives of the Federation; one representative of Republika Srpska; and two international members (including the Chairman) appointed by the President of the EBRD.

The Commission has established working groups in key sectors (power, railways, roads, water, post, and telecommunications). These working groups were requested to identify the difficulties and shortcomings of these public services of the Entities, as well as the regulatory and other problems to be solved in order to achieve proper power supply and proper communications within and between the Entities. Emphasis has been put on improving the coordination between the separate companies, rationality, and economic viability. Although a practical approach is being emphasized and priority is being given to short-term requirements and related arrangements, the ultimate objective of the Commission is clearly to propose long-term solutions and structures to the parties.

Sharing prewar assets and liabilities

Mutual recognition of infrastructure enterprises, including those of the two Federation utility companies, is still a highly political issue. In many cases, discussions on sharing debt burdens and other liabilities have not even been initiated. But, cooperation and coordination will be difficult unless these issues are resolved. The lack of coordination prevents efficient use of the remaining networks, especially when they cross Entity borders.[42]

Adjusting ownership and management of the utilities

All the utilities in Bosnia and Herzegovina are vertically integrated monopolies owned by government bodies and regulated and operated in the same way as in the former Yugoslavia. Government ownership has resulted in tight political control of the companies, from selection of management and strategic decision making to day-to-day activities. In this context, the financial situation of the companies, whether they operate as local utilities or national infrastructure systems, is generally unsatisfactory and sometimes critical.

Although the international community has provided significant financial support to repair war damage and restore service, investments in the years to come will have to be self-financed. Thus, international assistance to public utilities should shift from supporting emergency reconstruction to encouraging long-term cooperation and sectoral restructuring and reorganization. This goal can partly be achieved by implementing specific institution-building measures and by making government and donor support conditional on sectoral reform targets (including, but going beyond, financial viability). The donor community has extensive international experience in restructuring these sectors, and sharing this experience will prove enormously beneficial to both Entities. The experiences of Central and Eastern Europe and European Union guidelines should be particularly relevant, especially regarding concessions in

---

[42] Quantifying the losses due to this lack of coordination would be extremely difficult since reliable statistics are not available. However, observations made in other countries show that the costs to the economy that can result from improper management of infrastructure systems can reach 4 percent of GDP.

infrastructure projects (see Box 10.3). The current level of international assistance makes it possible for the authorities to implement needed reforms. Within the next year, appropriate plans for public utility reform should be developed with international cooperation and assistance.

Box 10.3 Infrastructure Concessions to the Private Sector

The case for concessions in infrastructure projects in Bosnia and Herzegovina is the same as what is generally advanced in other countries, i.e., mainly the potentially greater efficiency of the private sector, as compared to government institutions, to manage and operate projects, as well as the limited government resources which make financing by concessionaires hold out the promise of faster project implementation. At the same time, it should be recognized that concession agreements do not automatically provide the least-cost solution for provision of infrastructure.

International experience reveals a number of factors which are important for successful concessions:

sound project economic and financial viability;
manageable political risk;
fair public/private risk allocation; and
competent government organizations to conceive, prepare, and negotiate concession agreements.

While the general development which underlies the assessment of the above factors is moving in the right direction, it has to be recognized that presently the situation is far from ideal for concessions. Project viability has of course to be evaluated on a project-by-project basis, but for many of the projects mentioned as potential candidates (for example, motorways), it is evident that the basic conditions to ensure viability (traffic volumes, ability to pay) might still be questionable. Political risk, as well as the general capacity of government agencies to manage concessions, might make them difficult to implement at present.

Rebuilding the Power Sector

Before the war, Elektroprivreda Bosne i Hercegovine operated the electric-power system in Bosnia and Herzegovina. The system consisted of 13 hydropower plants with a total capacity of 2,034 megawatts (MW) and average annual output of 6,922 gigawatt hours (GWh), and 12 brown coal- and lignite-fired thermal power plants with an installed capacity of 1,957 megawatts and 10,675 gigawatts per year. The system had about 5,400 kilometers of transmission lines and 92,000 km of distribution lines.

The war destroyed more than half of generating capacity, 60 percent of the transmission network and control system, and most of the distribution network. In addition, the system was divided into Elektroprivreda Bosnia and Herzegovina (EPBosnia and Herzegovina) in the Bosniac-majority areas of the Federation, Elektroprivreda Herceg Bosne (EPHB) in the Croat-majority areas of the Federation; and Elektroprivreda Republika Srpska (EPRS) in Republika Srpska. Each company was made up of semiautonomous organizations, including several generation units (one for each power plant and associated coal mines, if any), one transmission unit (in each enterprise), and several distribution units (one for each distribution area).

At the end of the war, electricity companies faced the same problems as companies in other infrastructure sectors. The sector had been divided into three companies that do not coordinate or cooperate effectively, and that have not agreed on a division of assets and liabilities. Further, the companies have been losing a lot of money because of low tariffs, low billing and collection rates, and inefficient service.

Two reforms are essential

Better collection and higher tariffs. The power companies have extremely weak finances. The main problems are low billing and collection rates and low tariffs. In 1995, the power company in the Bosniac-majority areas of the Federation collected about 45 percent of the amount due, ranging from near zero in war-torn areas to close to prewar levels in unaffected area (these proportions may be misrepresented to the extent that vouchers are being accepted. In Republika Srpska, the power company collected only 39 percent of the amount due (54 percent in the Banja Luka area and 17 percent in the Pale area). Tariffs also vary by region, although they are low by international standards in all regions (Box 10.4).

Box 10.4 Electricity Tariffs in Bosnia and Herzegovina

Electricity tariffs vary significantly throughout the country. They are set by the utilities under the strict guidance of government authorities (and in Republika Srpska, on the basis of rates in the Federal Republic of Yugoslavia). Tariff information for Bosnia and Herzegovina and OECD countries is presented below.

Electric Power	Average Tariffs
Bosniac part of the Federation:	0.054 US$/kWh
Croat part of the Federation:	0.040 US$/kWh
Republika Srpska:	0.010 US$/kWh
OECD average	0.100 US$/kWh

More cooperation and closer coordination.. Although the electricity companies established in Republika Srpska and in the Croat-majority part of the Federation took over the assets of the prewar companies, they did not assume past debts and liabilities. It will be difficult to restore inter-Entity cooperation and to improve efficiency until this issue is resolved. Moreover, other republics of the former Yugoslavia built several major facilities as "investments in Bosnia and Herzegovina".[43] The authorities in Bosnia and Herzegovina and the successor organizations of these investors need to resolve the ownership issues relating to the facilities.

Although small infrastructure systems can be operated efficiently, it requires cooperation and power trading between neighboring networks. In Bosnia and Herzegovina, the large degree of prewar integration magnifies the need for cooperation: separating the services would be extremely expensive and might impair service quality in the short run, as well as jeopardize financial viability in the medium term.

Trading might be necessary because some areas lack power-generation capacity while others have a surplus. In the short term, guaranteeing sufficient and uninterrupted power supply will be possible only if the Entities trade with each other. For example, the situation in the Banja Luka area, which is currently supplied from the eastern part of Republika Srpska through a single unreliable transmission line crossing the Posavina corridor, could be significantly improved if Federation power companies also provided power. Inter-Entity trade and cooperation would not

---

[43] Such as the Ugljevik and Gacko thermal power plants, currently located in Republika Srpska, or the Tuzla and Kakanj thermal power plants, located in the Bosniac part of the Federation, which were partly owned by Croatia before the war.

require the companies to operate as a common network or to depend on common ownership and operating structures.

Restructuring should follow a three-stage approach

Although the power sector might not be large enough to allow competition even in generation, it is possible to develop a structure that would make it easier to attract potential investors (similar to successful measures in Poland and Hungary). Restructuring could proceed in three stages:

In the first stage, inter-Entity cooperation should be restored to optimize the use of existing infrastructure. Joint operational planning should be set up and repair works and reconstruction projects should be coordinated by the two Entities, even if investments and maintenance are managed separately.

In the second stage, generation should be separated from transmission and distribution and broken down into several generating companies, each operating on a commercial basis. Financial measures need to be taken to put each new company on sound financial footing while subsidies from government and other power companies are eliminated. The transmission system should be managed as a common system throughout the country to ensure the optimization of power transmission and permit effective power trading and system stabilization.[44] Distribution enterprises should be owned and operated on a regional basis, provided they are not too small to forgo important economies of scale. All companies should operate on a commercial basis. One option would be for the transmission company to buy power from the generating companies and sell it to the distribution companies, in which case transmission fees should not significantly exceed full cost recovery needs. A regulatory authority should be set up at the national level to regulate power prices and to ensure third-party access to the transmission system.

Finally, and only once the regulatory authority has been established and is operating with reasonable autonomy, the generation and distribution companies could be partly or totally privatized. The transmission company or companies could eventually be considered for privatization once the new ownership arrangements in the generation and distribution segments have stabilized. Regardless of whether the transmission network is privatized, the energy law should allow for third-party access to the network.

Developing a New Transportation System

Bosnia and Herzegovina's transport system was generally adequate before the war, with 8,600 km of main and regional roads, 1,030 km of railway lines (75 percent of it electrified), two civil airports, and public transportation services throughout the country. However, the war caused severe damage to the system and halted all maintenance. By the end of the war, more than 2,000 km of main roads needed immediate repair; 70 bridges, including all the bridges connecting Bosnia and Herzegovina to Croatia, needed to be rebuilt; all railway lines were

---

[44] Several options could be considered for the medium-term joint operation of the transmission network: a single transmission company (staffed with representatives of each company), separate companies with a common dispatching center (with or without dispatching subcenters), etc.

rendered inoperable; and Sarajevo airport was partly destroyed and closed to civilian traffic. Since the end of the war, road and railway links have been repaired and a small number of civilian charter flights have become available.

In the railway sector, as in the power sector, the prewar railway company was divided into three regional, government-owned companies: Zeljeznica Bosne i Herzegovine (ZBH) in the Bosniac-majority part of the Federation; Zeljeznica Herceg Bosne (ZHB) in the Croat-majority part of the Federation, and the Zeljeznice Transportovi Produzece Republike Srpske (ZTP) in Republika Srpska. Each company is responsible for investment, maintenance, and operations in its area.

Transport authorities must recognize two weaknesses

Tariffs are too low. Little information on pricing is available for the transport sector, although tariffs in the railways sector are quite low. A one-way passenger ticket from Doboj to Novi Grad (about 150 km), in Republika Srpska, costs US$3.50.

New taxes and closer coordination are needed. Road networks are owned and maintained by each Entity. Measures to ensure adequate financing of maintenance and investments still need to be worked out. Specific taxes, such as fuel taxes, should be established so that the authorities responsible for the road sector in each Entity have sufficient revenue to maintain and operate the road system.[45] Inter-Entity cooperation is also needed to ensure consistent reconstruction and investment programs and to carry out repairs along the Inter-Entity boundary line. Similar cooperation will be needed in the railways sector. Although cooperation has been partly established through a "Joint Board for Railways," it is still unsatisfactory (Box 10.5).

Railways should follow a two-stage restructuring strategy

The primary objective should be to open the rail network to all operating companies in two phases. First, each railway company should immediately be allowed to run trains on tracks owned by other companies without changing locomotives when entering a different area. In return, a fee would be paid for use of the network. Fees should be mutually acceptable and allow companies to fully recover costs. Contractual and economically based agreements should also be reached with the Croatian and the Serbian railways companies to ensure access to the European network and to address the cross-border lines (*e.g.,* Zagreb-Bihać-Knin-Split and Belgrade-Priboj-Podgorica).

In the second phase, investment and maintenance should be separated from operations, and investment and maintenance companies should be established at the Entity or canton level. Operation of the whole network should be authorized on a commercial basis (including payment of a uniform fee to the network companies). Third-party access to the network should be granted automatically.

---

[45] Such taxes already exist in the Croat-majority areas of the Federation. *They should be established as soon as possible in Republika Srpska and in the Bosniac-majority areas of the Federation.*

Box 10.5 Organization of the Railways

The network consists of two main axes :

North - South   (Croatia - Brcko - Tuzla - Doboj - Zenica - Sarajevo - Mostar - Ploce in Croatia)

West - East   (Croatia Novi Grad - Banja Luka - Doboj - Tuzla with a potential extension to Zvornik and Serbia).

Currently, due to severe war damage, only a very small part of this network is operating. Most connections between the main cities, once restored, could be operated by one or two companies. Operation of the inter-city lines would be as follows (distances are approximate):

Brcko - Tuzla	(75 km)	ZTP, ZBH
Novi Grad - Banja Luka	(80 km)	ZTP
Tuzla - Doboj	(60 km)	ZBH, ZTP
Banja Luka - Doboj	(100 km)	ZTP
Doboj - Zenica	(115 km)	ZTP, ZBH
Doboj - Tuzla	(60 km)	ZTP, ZBH
Zenica - Sarajevo	(80 km)	ZBH
(potentially) Tuzla - Zvornik	(50 km)	ZBH, ZTP
Sarajevo - Mostar	(120 km)	ZBH
Mostar - Ploce	(80 km)	ZBH, ZHB

Finally, better inter-Entity cooperation mechanisms are needed to address inter-Entity issues, and to decide on regulatory matters such as technical and operating standards (*e.g.*, telecommunications, signaling, security), the issuance of licenses to operating preexisting companies, coordination of time schedules and representation in technical international organizations.[46] While defining such arrangements, however, new structures should be created only to resolve identified issues. Once a proper regulatory framework has been put in place, the operating companies could be partly or totally privatized.

Building Viable Telecommunications Infrastructure

By the late 1980s, Bosnia and Herzegovina's telecommunications network was relatively modern, with a high degree of digitalization. Coverage was limited, however, with only 12 telephones for every 100 people. About 750,000 people were served by the several post and telecommunications enterprises (PTT), which were overseen by the Community of PTT enterprises of Bosnia and Herzegovina General Directorate. There were 6,000 international lines, including 700 direct links with countries outside the former Yugoslavia. Most international calls were routed through international telephone exchanges in Belgrade and Zagreb.

Heavy war damage of the long-distance transmission network disrupted interurban and international communications. By August 1996, more than 65 percent of the long-distance network had been destroyed, and 30 percent of local network lines were out of order. The European Bank for Reconstruction and Development estimated that the cost of restoring the

---

[46]   Several options could be considered for the development of inter-Entity coordination, for example, establishment of a railways authority at the national level or setup of working groups which would meet regularly, possibly through the Commission on Public Corporations.

sector, including rehabilitating the long-distance transmission network and procuring auxiliary equipment, would be about US$222 million.

As in the other sectors, the war split the PTT into three parts: PTT Bosne i Hercegovine (PTT Bosnia and Herzegovina) in the Bosniac-majority part of the Federation, and PTT Herceg Bosne (PTTHB) in the Croat-majority part of the Federation, and PTT Republika Srpske (PTTRS) in Republika Srpska. Each company consists of semi-autonomous regional or municipal organizations and is in charge of both post and telecommunications. PTTRS and PTTHB work very closely with the telecommunications companies of the Federal Republic of Yugoslavia and Croatia, respectively (their networks can be accessed from abroad only through the Yugoslav or Croatian country codes).

The issues are broadly similar to those in power and transport

Tariffs for local calls vary significantly even within ethnic majority areas (Box 10.6). However, the telecommunications companies are in better financial shape than other utilities because incoming and outgoing international calls generate revenue and a generally greater willingness (and ability) to pay for services.

Box 10.6 Tariffs for Local Calls	
Existing telephone rates in selected areas of the Federation are as follows:	
Sarajevo area	0.009 US$/minute
Bihać area	0.084 US$/minute
Croat-majority areas	0.006 US$/minute

Inter-Entity communications have been interrupted since the beginning of the war. In many areas, communications links could be restored without significant technical repairs, subject to an inter-Entity agreement. But since telecommunications is considered a strategic sector, cooperation between the PTTs is almost non existent and inter-Entity communications are limited to a few *red lines*. Even within the Federation, the Bosniac- and Croat-majority areas are hardly connected.

Reestablishing telecommunications services throughout Bosnia and Herzegovina, and with neighboring countries, is essential for economic revival. The three telecommunications companies should immediately reconnect their networks wherever technically possible, and service should be provided in a nondiscriminatory manner to all parts of the country.

The potential for privatization is greater than in other sectors

Telecommunications should be considered for rapid privatization, possibly with the involvement of foreign investors. To achieve this objective, measures to rapidly adapt the regulatory framework are needed, including:

- Separating postal services from telecommunications and establishing separate companies to deliver these services. Once established, these companies should have their own legal identity and keep accounts according to international standards and practices.

- Gradually opening up the sector to competition along the guidelines established by the European Union for its member countries. Measures should be worked out to move from the current monopolies to a situation where third-party access is granted.

- Establishing an independent regulatory body to issue licenses and ensure that operators respect existing regulations and contractual commitments.

Part Five

Normalizing External Flows Over the Medium Term

In 1996, the donor-financed reconstruction program has helped to boost GDP by about 50 percent. The expected initiation of the reconstruction program in Republika Srpska in 1997 should contribute to continued rapid economic recovery. Further improvements in economic performance will depend on a strong economic reform program, effective strengthening of institutional capacity for economic management, continued international financial and technical assistance, and, of course, continuated peace. If these conditions are maintained, Bosnia and Herzegovina should be able to recover nearly two thirds of prewar GDP by 2000. By 2003 or 2004, prewar GDP should be fully recovered.

Considerable external financing is needed to normalize Bosnia and Herzegovina's relations with international creditors and cover reconstruction requirements. This normalization involves both clearing outstanding arrears and servicing restructured debt. The strategy to resolve the debt problem should seek immediate relief on debt-service obligation as well as a permanent reduction of total indebtedness, thereby allowing the economy to function in both the short and medium term. Cash-flow relief on debt service from external donors is particularly important to assure a significant positive transfer into the country during recovery and to reduce the debt-service burden to a reasonable level. But, without an additional upfront reduction in the debt stock, the country will not be able to return to creditworthy status for some time, reducing any chance that private capital will be forthcoming to complement official aid.

Chapter XI

Medium-Term Economic Outlook
and External Financing Requirements

The Macroeconomic Outlook: Prospects for Growth

The momentum generated by the economic recovery of 1996 is expected to continue so long as peace, the reconstruction program, and progress in institution building and market reform are continued. Although, it is unlikely that growth in the medium term will be as rapid as in 1996 (50 percent), the growth rate in 1997 could still be 30-35 percent, bringing GDP per capita in 1997 to about US$1,000. Disposable GDP per capita could be higher still, at US$1,300, if citizens temporarily living abroad are not included in the population count.

As in 1996, sources of growth and employment generation in 1997 are expected to derive from the donor-financed reconstruction, and, to a lesser extent, from recovery in domestic markets and moderate growth in exports. Favorable factors in 1997 include the expected initiation of the reconstruction program in Republika Srpska, the strong pipeline of projects prepared for the Federation in 1996, that will be implemented in 1997, and initiation of a number of new projects. Economic recovery in the Federation in 1996 boosted demand for domestic output and imports. Other expected sources of growth include reconstruction in the housing and infrastructure sectors, the agricultural sector (particularly in Republika Srpska), the service sector (particularly in trade and food services) and to a lesser extent, the manufacturing sector (particularly the small-scale production of reconstruction materials, textiles, wood processing, and furniture making).

Beyond 1997, experience from other countries afflicted by war suggests that Bosnia and Herzegovina's economy still has the potential to grow very rapidly, although at declining rates. It is not unreasonable to assume that annual growth can be maintained at 10-25 percent during 1998-2000. *This growth scenario, however, requires the fulfillment of a number of conditions, including substantial reconstruction financing, debt relief from creditors, effective use of external assistance, and good progress in institution building and in implementation of economic reforms.* However, economic growth is starting from a very low base because of the war, the disintegration of former Yugoslavia, and changes in export markets as a result of the reorientation of Eastern European economies. Even under these growth assumptions, GDP after that will only reach, at most, about two thirds of its prewar level by 2000. After that, another three to four years will be needed before prewar GDP can be fully recovered (Table 11.1).

It will take even longer for exports to return to their prewar levels. Until basic infrastructure is rehabilitated and public services are restored, exports are unlikely to be a significant source of growth. As the economy recovers and domestic supply capacity is restored, some prewar export markets are expected to be regained. In real terms, exports are projected to recover from their current low base to about 70 percent of their prewar levels by 2000. Beyond the reconstruction phase, with significant recovery and easier access to inputs, labor, and capital, normal trade patterns might be restored, leading to a sizable improvement in the trade balance.

Based on these assumptions, the average trade deficit is projected to decline from about 30 percent of GDP during 1996-2000 to 6 percent in 2001-05 (see Table 11.1).

Table 11.1 Selected Key Economic Indicators: 1990-2005 [1]							(average)
	1990	**1995**	**1996**	**1997**	**1998**	**1999**	**2000** **2001-05**
I. Gross Domestic Product							
1. GDP (US$ billion)	10,633	2,105	3,260	4,500	5,900	7,300	8,500 11,540
2. Real GDP growth (%)	na	33	50	35	27	20	12 7
3. Per capita income (U.S.dollars)	2,429	501	776	1,079	1,412	1,745	2,013 2,748
II. External Trade Account							
1. Merchandise exports (US$ million)	1,990	152	336	702	1,042	1,395	1,796 2,778
2. Share of merchandise exports in GDP (%)	19	7	10	15	18	19	21 24
3. Merchandise imports (US$ million)	1,700	1,082	1,882	2,695	2,856	2,819	2,737 3,511
a. Reconstruction related	0	0	796	1,101	1,071	688	305 0
b. Humanitarian and in-kind aid	0	459	246	360	136	56	12 0
c. Other	1,700	623	840	1,234	1,649	2,075	2,420 3,375
4. Share of merchandise imports in GDP (%)	16	51	58	59	48	38	32 30
5. Trade balance (in percent of GDP)	3	-44	-47	-44	-31	-19	-11 -6
III. External Current Account							
1. Current account balance (in % of GDP)	na	-9	-26	-33	-25	-15	-6 -2
(excluding official transfers)	na	-27	-43	-38	-28	-16	-7 -2
V. International Reserves							
1. Total reserves (in months of imports)	na	2.4	3.2	3.2	3.8	4.1	4.5 4.0
IV. External Debt							
1. Total External Debt (in % of GDP)	na	168	115	58	53	46	41 63
2. Debt service (in % of total exports)	na	135	66	35	9	9	10 26

1/ 1990-96 are estimated; 1997-2005 are projected.

na: not available.

Note: The Bank scenario is illustrative, and it in no way is intended to prejudge the outcome of future negotiations with Bosnia's external creditors in the Paris and London Clubs. It shows that a comprehensive debt workout including a substantial net present value reduction on consolidated debt service with Paris Club creditors and a substantial debt stock reduction with London Club creditors goes a long way to create the conditions necessary for renewal of IBRD lending starting in 1998 and private capital inflows after 2000.

Source: Data provided by Bosnia and Herzegovina authorities, World Bank, and IMF staff estimates.

With successful implementation of the reform program, private investment is expected to increase more quickly than public investment in the years ahead. Public investments are needed to complement donor-supported reconstruction program in infrastructure, while private investments are expected in those sectors where capital requirements are relatively small and dependence on public infrastructure and services is limited. Given the tight monetary and fiscal rules needed to maintain macroeconomic stability, both public and private investments are expected to be financed, mostly, by external financial sources in the medium term. In time, domestic savings should increase, strengthening the performance of the financial sector. The savings and investment gap, however, will be slow to close, and external inflows will continue to play an important role in financing this gap. Given the front-loading of substantial donor assistance (including expected debt-rescheduling arrangements by creditors), official inflows are likely to decline after the reconstruction phase. Successful reforms will attract increasing private inflows, including equity financing.

External Financing Requirements Are Enormous

Bosnia and Herzegovina inherited substantial external debt (Table 11.2), much of which is in arrears (US$2 billion). Considerable external financing will be needed to normalize Bosnia and Herzegovina's relations with external creditors, as well as to cover the requirements of the reconstruction program. Normalization involves debt restructuring, including the clearance of outstanding arrears and servicing of the restructured debt. An important first step was taken on December 20, 1995, with the clearance of outstanding arrears owed to the International Monetary Fund. On June 14, 1996, the World Bank's Board of

Table 11.2 Estimated External Debt by Creditor (end 1995, in millions of U.S. dollars)		
Creditor	Outstanding Debt	In arrears
Multilateral	720	478
IBRD	625	447
IMF	49	0
Other	46	31
Paris Club	877	615
London Club	1,112	384
Other Creditors	809	502
Total	3,518	1,979

Executive Directors also approved a debt consolidation loan for Bosnia and Herzegovina that cleared its arrears to the Bank and reduced Bank-related debt-service requirements to normalize Bosnia's external financial relations.

Timely availability of international support will be of crucial importance in advancing economic recovery and transition. Working together, the government, the World Bank, the European Union, and other agencies have designed a reconstruction program requiring at least US$5.1 billion of external financing during 1996-99 period. This program has since been endorsed by the donor community, which in 1996 committed about US$1.8 billion to specific sectoral programs (reaching the original targets). About 96 percent of this funding was provided on grant or concessional terms. Of the US$1.8 billion committed, 65 percent is being used to support the priority reconstruction program, including civil works, services, equipment and goods contracts, and balance-of-payments support. In 1996, reconstruction efforts focused largely on the Federation.

The 1997 program should focus on infrastructure, refugee return, employment generation, and overall sustainability of the program. The first year's assistance was provided on an emergency basis, with less attention to long-term policy issues; from now on, both the government and donors should be increasingly conscious of the need to ensure the long-term viability of their interventions. External financing requirements have been established on the basis of a sector-by-sector assessment of future needs, taking into account both the status of reconstruction-program implementation during 1996 and Bosnia and Herzegovina's absorptive capacity.

The External Debt Problem Must Be Addressed

Bosnia and Herzegovina's unsustainable debt indicators originate from the collapse of its economy over the past four years. GDP declined from US$10.6 billion in 1990 to about US$2.1 billion in 1995, and total exports (including those to other former Yugoslav republics) dropped from US$2 billion to about US$150 million during the same period. Debt indicators in 1995 were very poor: the country's ratio of debt to GDP was 168 percent, and the ratio of required debt service to total exports was about 135 percent. Even with strong recovery and a 1996 workout agreement with creditors covering some debt, these indicators remain prohibitively high. Bosnia and Herzegovina is clearly in no position to service this debt now or in the near future.

Debt restructuring is unavoidable. An effective solution would include two elements. First, Bosnia and Herzegovina is in no position to make net payments for several years to come. Thus *cash-flow relief* is needed to ensure a strongly positive net transfer into Bosnia and Herzegovina. Second, once foreign assistance declines, access to private capital markets needs to be secured to ensure continued recovery. Renewed access to private markets is unlikely with the current stock of debt (the current ratio of debt to GDP is more than twice as high as Mexico was before its Brady debt-restructuring deal). Thus, debt restructuring needs to provide not only cash-flow relief, but also significant *debt relief* to lower the debt-output ratio to serviceable levels. Without prejudging any final settlement that might be reached with the Paris and London Clubs, a comprehensive workout would contribute significantly to creating the conditions needed to restore creditworthiness and permit private inflows to contribute to reconstruction efforts in later years.

An Illustrative Scenario for External Financing

The illustrative scenario presented here is in no way intended to prejudge the outcome of future negotiations with Bosnia and Herzegovina's external creditors in the Paris and London Clubs. It shows, however, that a comprehensive debt workout, including a substantial reduction in consolidated debt service and debt stock would go a long way toward creating the conditions needed to reestablish Bosnia and Herzegovina's creditworthiness and to grant its access to international resources at commercial or near-commercial terms. Less generous terms would leave Bosnia and Herzegovina's creditworthiness more fragile and access to such flows in question. This illustrative scenario takes into account financial normalization packages offered by international financial institutions in 1995-96 and is based on two assumptions:

- Clearance of pre-cutoff date arrears to Paris Club creditors in mid-1997, on Naples terms, (that is a two-third net present value reduction on consolidated debt service, and a deferral, on an exceptional basis, of post-cutoff date debt arrears over a six-year period, including three years of grace).

- A deeper net present value debt reduction than under Naples terms, at about 80 percent,[47] by London Club creditors and rescheduling of all debt to other creditors on Naples terms, with a 67 percent net present value reduction by the end of 1997.

Under this scenario, Bosnia and Herzegovina's gross external financing needs will total about US$12.4 billion during the period 1996-2000 (Table 11.3). Most (60 percent) of this amount comes from the current-account deficit, which is largely driven by reconstruction needs, and from other import requirements (humanitarian imports and private sector imports). The next largest component of the financing needs (about 22 percent) is accounted for by arrears clearance (US$2.7 billion). Debt service on rescheduled and new debt to multilateral and Paris Club

---

[47] Comprises a 90 percent discount assumed for half of the debt, which is assumed to be bought back at around 10 cents on the dollar, and a rescheduling of the remainder on Naples terms with a net present value reduction of 67 percent. The buy-back component would require financing of about US$65 million which contributes to the financing gap in 1997.

creditors accounts for about US$0.7 billion or 5 percent of the financing requirement. Debt service to London Club and other commercial creditors, including rollover of debt service in 1997, accounts for 0.6 billion, or 5 percent of the financing requirement. Finally, the accumulation of international reserves to a precautionary level accounts for about US$0.9 billion, or 7 percent of the financing requirements.

These needs are projected to be met through a combination of sources. About US$3 billion (31 percent) is expected to be provided through official and private unrequited transfers. Official unrequited transfers should decline over time as humanitarian assistance is replaced by reconstruction assistance on concessional terms. Private unrequited transfers should also fall over time, reflecting its two components: emergency assistance needs that are currently addressed by nongovernmental organizations, which are assumed to decline over time, and private remittances from Bosnian families working abroad, which are expected to remain constant. Foreign direct investment inflows are expected to resume in 1998 and to provide about US$0.5 billion in financing .

New financing for the reconstruction and recovery program (about US$5.1 billion) would cover 54 percent of the total financing requirement. These funds will come from various creditors, mostly on concessional terms. In addition, multilateral creditors, bilateral creditors (including Paris Club creditors), and commercial creditors (including London Club creditors) will finance about 64 percent of the remaining US$4 billion financing gap by forgiving arrears. The remaining financing gap for the four-year period is about US$0.7 billion, averaging about US$170 million a year, or 6 percent of total financing requirements. This remaining financing gap will be covered by balance of payments support from the World Bank, IMF, other multilateral creditors, and bilateral creditors. It bears repeating, however, that the calculation of the remaining financing gap *assumes that financing for the reconstruction program has already been fully secured, and that a comprehensive debt workout has contributed to substantial debt relief as mentioned above.*

This debt workout scenario illustrates how debt service relief and debt stock reduction can help restore country creditworthiness. Under the scenario, overall debt parameters would indicate a substantial decline in debt and debt-service indicators. For example, the ratio of debt to GDP would fall from 168 percent in 1995 to about 41 percent by 2000, and the composition of debt stock will be more favorable in terms of the degree of concessionality of the debt terms.

With such a strategy, it is possible that a viable medium-term economic program, based on restoration of country creditworthiness and renewed access to international capital markets, can be realistically envisaged and, thus, sustained growth can be expected. Less generous terms would, of course, have a weaker impact, and imply slower growth.

Table 11.3 External Financing Requirements: 1995-2000[1]							
(millions of US dollars)							
	1995	**1996**	**1997**	**1998**	**1999**	**2000**	**96-2000**
I. Financing needs	*1,645*	*3,071*	*4,759*	*2,130*	*1,535*	*944*	*12,439*
1. Current account deficit excluding interest and transfers	953	1,620	2,084	1814	1,286	658	7,462
2. Debt service to multilateral and Paris Club creditors	274	185	99	108	141	203	736
a. On existing debt	274	182	87	80	97	152	598
b. On new debt	0	3	12	28	44	51	138
3. Debt service to London Club and other commercial creditors[2]	242	248	294	33	33	33	641
4. Arrears clearance[3]	38	620	2,057	0	0	0	2,677
5. Change in gross reserves (+:increase)	138	398	225	175	75	50	923
II. Financing sources	*1,645*	*3,071*	*2,221*	*1980*	*1,432*	*845*	*9,549*
1. Unrequited net transfers	1,002	1,094	781	480	354	297	3,006
a. Official	377	558	421	190	100	60	1,329
b. Private	625	536	360	290	254	237	1,677
2. New financing for reconstruction[4]	0	1,040	1,440	1,400	901	371	5,152
a. Official transfers for reconstruction	0	796	1,102	1,071	689	230	3,888
b. New medium- and long-term capital inflows	0	244	338	329	212	141	1,264
3. World Bank Consolidation Loan	0	620	0	0	0	0	620
4. Foreign direct investment	0	0	0	100	200	200	500
5. Exceptional financing	478	354	0	0	0	0	354
6. Others[5]	165	-37		0	-23	-23	-83
III. Financing gap	*0*	*0*	*2,538*	*150*	*103*	*99*	*2,890*
1. Arrears clearance and debt relief	0	0	2,200	0	0	0	2,200
a. Rollover/debt relief, London Club and other commercial creditors	0	0	1519	0	0	0	1,519
b. Clearance of arrears to Paris Club	0	0	681	0	0	0	681
2. Remaining financing gap[6]	0	0	338	150	103	99	690
IV. Memo items							
1. Total external debt/GDP (%)	168	115	58	53	46	41	63
2. Debt service/Total exports (%)[7]	135	66	35	9	9	10	26

[1] 1995-96 are estimated; 1997-2000 are projected.

[2] Assumes rollover of debt service in 1997 (i.e., accumulation of arrears) and debt service at terms comparable to Naples terms thereafter.

[3] Includes clearance of arrears to the IBRD and assumes clearance of arrears to other multilateral and bilateral creditors, including the
Paris Club, by mid-97 and to the London Club and other commercial creditors by end-1997.

[4] Assumes that financing of the reconstruction program is fully secured.

[5] Includes use of IMF resources (US$45 million), errors, and omissions.

[6] After clearance of arrears to multilateral creditors, Paris Club, London Club and other commercial creditors, but before balance of payments financing from the World Bank, the IMF, other multilateral creditors, and bilateral creditors.

[7] 1995 figure refers to scheduled debt service. 1996 figure includes debt service to the IBRD at new terms and scheduled but unpaid non-IBRD debt service.

Note: This scenario is illustrative, and is in no way intended to prejudge the outcome of future negotiations with Bosnia and Herzegovina's external creditors in the Paris and the London Clubs. It shows that a comprehensive debt workout, including a substantial net present value reduction on the consolidated service with Paris Club creditors and a substantial debt stock reduction with London Club creditors would go a long way toward creating the conditions necessary for renewal of IBRD lending starting in 1998 and private capital inflows after 2000.

Source: Data provided by Bosnia and Herzegovina authorities, the IMF, and World Bank staff estimates.

Bibliography

Bosnia and Herzegovina. Various Issues. *Statistical Data on Economic and Social Trends.* Sarajevo: Institute of Statistics of Bosnia and Herzegovina.

Ding, Wei, 1991. *Yugoslavia: Costs and Benefits of Union and Interdependence of Regional Economies.* Comparative Economic Studies Vol. XXXIII, no. 4. Michigan: Association for Comparative Economic Studies.

Fox, William and Christine Wallich. January, 1997. *Fiscal Federalism in Bosnia-Herzegovina: The Dayton Challenge.* Washington, DC: World Bank - Policy Research Working Paper no. WPS1714.

International Monetary Fund. *Recent Economic Developments.* Washington, DC: IMF, Various Issues.

The World Bank and The European Bank for Reconstruction and Development. September 28, 1995. *Bosnia and Herzegovina: Priorities for Recovery and Growth.* Washington, DC: World Bank.

The World Bank. September 29, 1995. *Bosnia and Herzegovina: Economic Issues and Priorities.* Washington, DC: World Bank.

The World Bank and The European Bank for Reconstruction and Development. April 2, 1996. *Bosnia and Herzegovina, The Priority Reconstruction and Recovery Program: The Challenges Ahead.* Washington, DC: World Bank.

The World Bank, The European Bank for Reconstruction and Development, and The European Commission. 1996. *Bosnia and Herzegovina: Toward Economic Recovery.* Washington, DC: World Bank.

The World Bank, The European Bank for Reconstruction and Development, and The European Commission. November, 1996. *Bosnia and Herzegovina: The Priority Reconstruction Program, From Emergency to Sustainability.* Three volumes. Washington, DC: World Bank.

The World Bank, and The European Bank for Reconstruction and Development. Three issues dated July 1996, December 1996, and January 1997. *Bosnia and Herzegovina: The Priority Reconstruction Program, Sectoral Projects and Programs.* Washington, DC: World Bank.

The World Bank. February 1997. *Private Sector Development in Post-War Bosnia-Herzegovina.* Washington, DC: World Bank.

Distributors of World Bank Publications

Prices and credit terms vary from country to country. Consult your local distributor before placing an order.

ARGENTINA
Oficina del Libro Internacional
Av. Cordoba 1877
1120 Buenos Aires
Tel: (54 1) 815-8354
Fax: (54 1) 815-8156

AUSTRALIA, FIJI, PAPUA NEW GUINEA, SOLOMON ISLANDS, VANUATU, AND WESTERN SAMOA
D.A. Information Services
648 Whitehorse Road
Mitcham 3132
Victoria
Tel: (61) 3 9210 7777
Fax: (61) 3 9210 7788
E-mail: service@dadirect.com.au
URL: http://www.dadirect.com.au

AUSTRIA
Gerold and Co.
Weihburggasse 26
A-1011 Wien
Tel: (43 1) 512-47-31-0
Fax: (43 1) 512-47-31-29
URL: http://www.gerold.co/at.online

BANGLADESH
Micro Industries Development Assistance Society (MIDAS)
House 5, Road 16
Dhanmondi R/Area
Dhaka 1209
Tel: (880 2) 326427
Fax: (880 2) 811188

BELGIUM
Jean De Lannoy
Av. du Roi 202
1060 Brussels
Tel: (32 2) 538-5169
Fax: (32 2) 538-0841

BRAZIL
Publicações Tecnicas Internacionais Ltda.
Rua Peixoto Gomide, 209
01409 Sao Paulo, SP.
Tel: (55 11) 259-6644
Fax: (55 11) 258-6990
E-mail: postmaster@pti.uol.br
URL: http://www.uol.br

CANADA
Renouf Publishing Co. Ltd.
5369 Canotek Road
Ottawa, Ontario K1J 9J3
Tel: (613) 745-2665
Fax: (613) 745-7660
E-mail: renouf@fox.nstn.ca
URL: http://www.fox.nstn.ca/~renouf

CHINA
China Financial & Economic Publishing House
8, Da Fo Si Dong Jie
Beijing
Tel: (86 10) 6333-8257
Fax: (86 10) 6401-7365

COLOMBIA
Infoenlace Ltda.
Carrera 6 No. 51-21
Apartado Aereo 34270
Santafé de Bogotá, D.C.
Tel: (57 1) 285-2798
Fax: (57 1) 285-2798

COTE D'IVOIRE
Center d'Edition et de Diffusion Africaines (CEDA)
04 B.P. 541
Abidjan 04
Tel: (225) 24 6510;24 6511
Fax: (225) 25 0567

CYPRUS
Center for Applied Research
Cyprus College
6, Diogenes Street, Engomi
P.O. Box 2006
Nicosia
Tel: (357 2) 44-1730
Fax: (357 2) 46-2051

CZECH REPUBLIC
National Information Center
prodejna, Konviktska 5
CS – 113 57 Prague 1
Tel: (42 2) 2422-9433
Fax: (42 2) 2422-1484
URL: http://www.nis.cz/

DENMARK
SamfundsLitteratur
Rosenoerns Allé 11
DK-1970 Frederiksberg C
Tel: (45 31) 351942
Fax: (45 31) 357822

EGYPT, ARAB REPUBLIC OF
Al Ahram Distribution Agency
Al Galaa Street
Cairo
Tel: (20 2) 578-6083
Fax: (20 2) 578-6833

The Middle East Observer
41, Sherif Street
Cairo
Tel: (20 2) 393-9732
Fax: (20 2) 393-9732

FINLAND
Akateeminen Kirjakauppa
P.O. Box 128
FIN-00101 Helsinki
Tel: (358 0) 12141
Fax: (358 0) 121-4441
URL: http://www.akateeminen.com/

FRANCE
World Bank Publications
66, avenue d'Iéna
75116 Paris
Tel: (33 1) 40-69-30-56/57
Fax: (33 1) 40-69-30-68

GERMANY
UNO-Verlag
Poppelsdorfer Allee 55
53115 Bonn
Tel: (49 228) 212940
Fax: (49 228) 217492

GREECE
Papasotiriou S.A.
35, Stournara Str.
106 82 Athens
Tel: (30 1) 364-1826
Fax: (30 1) 364-8254

HAITI
Culture Diffusion
5, Rue Capois
C.P. 257
Port-au-Prince
Tel: (509 1) 3 9260

HONG KONG, MACAO
Asia 2000 Ltd.
Sales & Circulation Department
Seabird House, unit 1101-02
22-28 Wyndham Street, Central
Hong Kong
Tel: (852) 2530-1409
Fax: (852) 2526-1107
E-mail: sales@asia2000.com.hk
URL: http://www.asia2000.com.hk

INDIA
Allied Publishers Ltd.
751 Mount Road
Madras - 600 002
Tel: (91 44) 852-3938
Fax: (91 44) 852-0649

INDONESIA
Pt. Indira Limited
Jalan Borobudur 20
P.O. Box 181
Jakarta 10320
Tel: (62 21) 390-4290
Fax: (62 21) 421-4289

IRAN
Ketab Sara Co. Publishers
Khaled Eslamboli Ave.,
6th Street
Kusheh Delafrooz No. 8
Tehran
Tel: (98 21) 8717819; 8716104
Fax: (98 21) 8712479
E-mail: ketab-sara@neda.net.ir

Kowkab Publishers
P.O. Box 19575-511
Tehran
Tel: (98 21) 258-3723
Fax: (98 21) 258-3723

IRELAND
Government Supplies Agency
Oifig an tSoláthair
4-5 Harcourt Road
Dublin 2
Tel: (353 1) 661-3111
Fax: (353 1) 475-2670

ISRAEL
Yozmot Literature Ltd.
P.O. Box 56055
3 Yohanan Hasandlar Street
Tel Aviv 61560
Tel: (972 3) 5285-397
Fax: (972 3) 5285-397

R.O.Y. International
PO Box 13056
Tel Aviv 61130
Tel: (972 3) 5461423
Fax: (972 3) 5461442
E-mail: royil@netvision.net.il

Palestinian Authority/Middle East
Index Information Services
P.O.B. 19502 Jerusalem
Tel: (972 2) 6271219
Fax: (972 2) 6271634

ITALY
Licosa Commissionaria Sansoni SPA
Via Duca Di Calabria, 1/1
Casella Postale 552
50125 Firenze
Tel: (55) 645-415
Fax: (55) 641-257
E-mail: licosa@ftbcc.it
Url: http://www.ftbcc.it//licosa

JAMAICA
Ian Randle Publishers Ltd.
206 Old Hope Road
Kingston 6
Tel: 809-927-2085
Fax: 809-977-0243
E-mail: irpl@colis.com

JAPAN
Eastern Book Service
3-13 Hongo 3-chome, Bunkyo-ku
Tokyo 113
Tel: (81 3) 3818-0861
Fax: (81 3) 3818-0864
E-mail: svt-ebs@ppp.bekkoame.or.jp
URL: http://www.bekkoame.or.jp/~svt-ebs

KENYA
Africa Book Service (E.A.) Ltd.
Quaran House, Mfangano Street
P.O. Box 45245
Nairobi
Tel: (254 2) 223 641
Fax: (254 2) 330 272

KOREA, REPUBLIC OF
Daejon Trading Co. Ltd.
P.O. Box 34, Youida
706 Seoun Bldg
44-6 Youido-Dong, Yeongchengo-Ku
Seoul
Tel: (82 2) 785-1631/4
Fax: (82 2) 784-0315

MALAYSIA
University of Malaya Cooperative
Bookshop, Limited
P.O. Box 1127
Jalan Pantai Baru
59700 Kuala Lumpur
Tel: (60 3) 756-5000
Fax: (60 3) 755-4424

MEXICO
INFOTEC
Av. San Fernando No. 37
Col. Toriello Guerra
14050 Mexico, D.F.
Tel: (52 5) 624-2800
Fax: (52 5) 624-2822
E-mail: infotec@rtn.net.mx
URL: http://rtn.net.mx

NEPAL
Everest Media International Services (P)Ltd.
GPO Box 5443
Kathmandu
Tel: (977 1) 472 152
Fax: (977 1) 224 431

NETHERLANDS
De Lindeboom/InOr-Publikaties
P.O. Box 202
7480 AE Haaksbergen
Tel: (31 53) 574-0004
Fax: (31 53) 572-9296
E-mail: lindeboo@worldonline.nl
URL: http://www.worldonline.nl/~lindeboo

NEW ZEALAND
EBSCO NZ Ltd.
Private Mail Bag 99914
New Market
Auckland
Tel: (64 9) 524-8119
Fax: (64 9) 524-8067

NIGERIA
University Press Limited
Three Crowns Building Jericho
Private Mail Bag 5095
Ibadan
Tel: (234 22) 41-1356
Fax: (234 22) 41-2056

NORWAY
NIC Info A/S
Book Department
P.O. Box 6125 Etterstad
N-0602 Oslo 6
Tel: (47 22) 57-3300
Fax: (47 22) 68-1901

PAKISTAN
Mirza Book Agency
65, Shahrah-e-Quaid-e-Azam
Lahore 54000
Tel: (92 42) 735 3601
Fax: (92 42) 758 5283

Oxford University Press
5 Bangalore Town
Sharae Faisal
PO Box 13033
Karachi-75350
Tel: (92 21) 446307
Fax: (92 21) 4547640
E-mail: oup@oup.khi.erum.com.pk

Pak Book Corporation
Aziz Chambers 21
Queen's Road
Lahore
Tel: (92 42) 636 3222; 636 0885
Fax: (92 42) 636 2328
E-mail: pbc@brain.net.pk

PERU
Editorial Desarrollo SA
Apartado 3824
Lima 1
Tel: (51 14) 285380
Fax: (51 14) 286628

PHILIPPINES
International Booksource Center Inc.
1127-A Antipolo St.
Barangay, Venezuela
Makati City
Tel: (63 2) 896 6501; 6505; 6507
Fax: (63 2) 896 1741

POLAND
International Publishing Service
Ul. Piekna 31/37
00-677 Warzawa
Tel: (48 2) 628-6089
Fax: (48 2) 621-7255
E-mail: books%ips@ikp.atm.com.pl
URL: http://www.ipscg.waw.pl/ips/export/

PORTUGAL
Livraria Portugal
Apartado 2681
Rua Do Carmo 70-74
1200 Lisbon
Tel: (1) 347-4982
Fax: (1) 347-0264

ROMANIA
Compani De Librarii Bucuresti S.A.
Str. Lipscani no. 26, sector 3
Bucharest
Tel: (40 1) 613 9645
Fax: (40 1) 312 4000

RUSSIAN FEDERATION
Isdatelstvo <Ves Mir>
9a, Lolpachniy Pereulok
Moscow 101831
Tel: (7 095) 917 87 49
Fax: (7 095) 917 92 59

SINGAPORE, TAIWAN, MYANMAR, BRUNEI
Ashgate Publishing Asia Pacific Pte. Ltd.
41 Kallang Pudding Road #04-03
Golden Wheel Building
Singapore 349316
Tel: (65) 741-5166
Fax: (65) 742-9356
E-mail: ashgate@asianconnect.com

SLOVENIA
Gospodarski Vestnik Publishing Group
Dunajska cesta 5
1000 Ljubljana
Tel: (386 61) 133 83 47; 132 12 30
Fax: (386 61) 133 80 30
E-mail: belicd@gvestnik.si

SOUTH AFRICA, BOTSWANA
For single titles:
Oxford University Press Southern Africa
P.O. Box 1141
Cape Town 8000
Tel: (27 21) 45-7266
Fax: (27 21) 45-7265

For subscription orders:
International Subscription Service
P.O. Box 41095
Craighall
Johannesburg 2024
Tel: (27 11) 880-1448
Fax: (27 11) 880-6248
E-mail: iss@is.co.za

SPAIN
Mundi-Prensa Libros, S.A.
Castello 37
28001 Madrid
Tel: (34 1) 431-3399
Fax: (34 1) 575-3998
E-mail: libreria@mundiprensa.es
URL: http://www.mundiprensa.es/

Mundi-Prensa Barcelona
Consell de Cent, 391
08009 Barcelona
Tel: (34 3) 488-3492
Fax: (34 3) 487-7659
E-mail: barcelona@mundiprensa.es

SRI LANKA, THE MALDIVES
Lake House Bookshop
100, Sir Chittampalam Gardiner Mawatha
Colombo 2
Tel: (94 1) 32105
Fax: (94 1) 432104

SWEDEN
Wennergren-Williams AB
P.O. Box 1305
S-171 25 Solna
Tel: (46 8) 705-97-50
Fax: (46 8) 27-00-71
E-mail: mail@wwi.se

SWITZERLAND
Librairie Payot Service Institutionnel
Côtes-de-Montbenon 30
1002 Lausanne
Tel: (41 21) 341-3229
Fax: (41 21) 341-3235

ADECO Van Diemen EditionsTechniques
Ch. de Lacuez 41
CH1807 Blonay
Tel: (41 21) 943 2673
Fax: (41 21) 943 3605

TANZANIA
Oxford University Press
Maktaba Street
PO Box 5299
Dar es Salaam
Tel: (255 51) 29209
Fax: (255 51) 46822

THAILAND
Central Books Distribution
306 Silom Road
Bangkok 10500
Tel: (66 2) 235-5400
Fax: (66 2) 237-8321

TRINIDAD & TOBAGO, AND THE CARRIBBEAN
Systematics Studies Unit
9 Watts Street
Curepe
Trinidad, West Indies
Tel: (809) 662-5654
Fax: (809) 662-5654
E-mail: tobe@trinidad.net

UGANDA
Gustro Ltd.
PO Box 9997, Madhvani Building
Plot 16/4 Jinja Rd.
Kampala
Tel: (256 41) 254 763
Fax: (256 41) 251 468

UNITED KINGDOM
Microinfo Ltd.
P.O. Box 3
Alton, Hampshire GU34 2PG
England
Tel: (44 1420) 86848
Fax: (44 1420) 89889
E-mail: wbank@ukminfo.demon.co.uk
URL: http://www.microinfo.co.uk

VENEZUELA
Tecni-Ciencia Libros, S.A.
Centro Cuidad Comercial Tamanco
Nivel C2
Caracas
Tel: (58 2) 959 5547; 5035; 0016
Fax: (58 2) 959 5636

ZAMBIA
University Bookshop, University of Zambia
Great East Road Campus
P.O. Box 32379
Lusaka
Tel: (260 1) 252 576
Fax: (260 1) 253 952

ZIMBABWE
Longman Zimbabwe (Pte.)Ltd.
Tourle Road, Ardbennie
P.O. Box ST125
Southerton
Harare
Tel: (263 4) 6216617
Fax: (263 4) 621670

03/10/97